# Show Me The Math:
## The importance of cost estimates when engaging a law firm

AF744112

RICHARD BRZAKALA

**Commissioning editor**
Alex Davies

**Published by**
Globe Law and Business Ltd
3 Mylor Close
Horsell
Woking
Surrey GU21 4DD
United Kingdom
Tel: +44 20 3745 4770
www.globelawandbusiness.com

ISBN: 978-1-78358-396-6
A catalogue record for this book is available from the British Library

© Originally published by Ark Group 2020
© 2021 Globe Law and Business Ltd except where otherwise indicated

All rights reserved. No part of this publication may be reproduced or transmitted in any form or by any means, except in accordance with the provisions of the Copyright, Designs and Patents Act 1988 or under terms of a licence issued by the Copyright Licencing Agency in respect of photocopying and/or reprographic reproduction. Application for permission for other use of copyright material, including permission to reproduce extracts in other published works, should be made in writing to the publishers. Full acknowledgement of author, publisher, and source must be given.

DISCLAIMER
This publication is intended as a general guide only. The information and opinions it contains are not intended to provide legal advice. The publishers bear no responsibility for any errors or omissions contained herein.

# Contents

# Executive Summary

Gone are the days when a law firm would provide their corporate client with a cost estimate for a matter that was based solely on subjective "gut" feelings and nothing more. Over my 20 years of legal operations experience, I have heard many partners at many firms say a variation of such things as "business people are not lawyers, so they don't understand the nuances of the law and how we price our work", that clients "don't have our (legal) intuitive experience" or that "the legal work is bespoke, complicated and has too many variables to put into a cost estimate". Over the past decade, an increasing intolerance has been building amongst the corporate community against such dismissive and diminutive comments.

I have worked with numerous general counsels, senior executives, and business clients at various companies on many different cost savings, control and effectiveness initiatives – all aimed at interpreting and leveraging cost and billing data to create savings. The corporate constituency will continue to use their buying power and control demand for legal services in the new legal marketplace that emerges post-pandemic 2020. Once the world returns to a new economic (near) normal, corporate clients will be increasingly looking to firms for objective and analytical cost estimates that are well thought out and supported by a clear understanding of what the client wants.

I expect that in the post-pandemic marketplace, the economic pressures facing clients today to control or reduce legal spend, generate cost savings and/or create operational efficiencies will only intensify. Consequently, clients will be forced to increase the scrutiny of their legal service providers, especially how they deliver their services.

Since the recession of 2008, law firms have increasingly begun to look inwards at their cost structures, business processes, and operations with a view to cut costs, invest in technology, and reduce margins to protect profits. Economic rationalization and efficiency practices will only intensify in the post-pandemic legal marketplace as firms will increasingly be challenged to manage and maintain market share and profitability in the face of hyper-competitiveness and a marketplace that may inevitably contract because of an impending global recession.

Therefore, because many firms today are already increasingly having to work smarter and more efficiently, clients expect that all of the efficiency and cost saving projects that firms undertake should translate into more affordable legal services for clients and that those savings should show up in the cost estimates that firms put forward.

Excellent legal advice and service delivery have always been and continue to be present in the requirements that many clients impose on the firms they engage. But just as important is the need for transparency when it comes to how a firm prices its legal services. Therefore, what better title for a book that discusses the importance of cost estimates then "Show me the math" – as I have asked this many times working with law firms around the world. I have also heard the same request coming from many other clients, so much so, that I think it has become the mantra of the corporate community that continues to search for constant assurance that they are paying a fair price and receiving value for the work that firms deliver. In my experience the value that is derived from the transparency that a client gains from a firm's cost estimate is invaluable. If done right, clients get to understand not only how a law firm calculates the price of a matter, but also whether the firm understands the scope of the engagement, the utilization of its resources (staffing), the quantity of time each professional is expected to work on the matter, the cost for specific tasks or key deliverables, and how variances and assumptions will be dealt with if they should materialize. All of these individual components sum up to provide the client with the price in a cost estimate, but also help to provide an assurance of how the legal services and value of a matter will be delivered. I believe clients today want to see what is behind the "magic curtain" so to speak. "Show me the math" is another way of asking for greater transparency, an assurance that what the client receives from its law firm is backed up by real historical data, expertise, and experience and not just subjective or gut feelings. Clients see this level of transparency (i.e. backed up by real data) as synonymous with honesty and trust.

*Show me the math* walks the reader through a comprehensive analysis of all of the components of a successful cost estimate strategy. My intention in writing this book was not to create an instruction manual but instead to share my thoughts, experiences and what I have seen as best practices when it comes to cost estimate strategies and their importance in today's legal marketplace for both the client and the legal service provider. This book can help corporate clients, lawyers, legal operations experts, law firm CFOs, CMOs and finance experts to develop cost estimate strategies, increase efficiency, lower costs, and improve client/law firm relationships by understanding how value can be measured and monitored through the utilization of cost estimate tools and strategies. I have also spoken to numerous young lawyers, fresh out of law school, who have struggled with working with cost estimates. I hope this book can help those who may still be studying in law school with a better understanding of what corporate clients are looking for in terms of cost estimate proposals.

Whenever possible I have tried to address cost estimate strategies from both the client's perspective as well as the firm's, and highlight the pros and cons to the topic that is being presented.

I have divided the book into five principal chapters, starting with the benefits of a cost estimate, where I provide a detailed narrative around the benefits of cost estimate strategies and the attraction and increased popularity of cost estimates amongst corporate clients. The marketplace today and in all probability post-2020 will continue to be driven by clients looking for any and every opportunity to control legal costs. Understanding the benefits for clients, as well as firms, helps set the table for those parties looking to implement a cost-saving strategy or reinforce existing strategies that may be faltering due to user acceptance.

In chapter two, I review a variety of topics around cost estimate strategies but begin with the importance of different pricing models that clients are attracted to when engaging law firms on cost estimates. Although there has been a huge market push to move away from the hourly rate model, it continues to be the basis for many clients and law firms in calculating their cost estimates proposals. I look at the different AFA options that clients utilize and question the value of law firms continuing to utilize commercial (street) rates and ambiguous dollar ranges in the cost proposals that they propose to their clients.

I continue my analysis with a focus on how firms should leverage all of their internal resources, historical data and especially their legal operation folks when working on a client's cost estimate. Once upon a time, it used to be a couple of lawyers in a board room with a billing clerk working on a cost estimate that was based mostly on intuition and some data. However, today clients expect to see real data backed up by real historical experience. They want to see and understand a law firm's efficiency ratio, whether a firm staffs its matters partner- or associate-heavy (i.e. staffing ratio), or how a firm measures its work in progress (WIP ratio) relative to an agreed budget amount. I also focus on the law firm efficiency and clients' expectations with regards to firms increasingly having to work smarter and more efficiently. All of these components are discussed in chapter two, as are the changes that are taking place with the traditional legal model.

Communication and proper scope definition are two areas where clients, as well as law firms, have struggled to get "it" right and that are perhaps areas that can have the biggest impact on both parties to a cost estimate agreement. In chapter two, I highlight this section and the importance of defining scope at the outset of a matter and how firms should not shy away from challenging clients if the scope is not defined properly. When things do go wrong, such as in an overage situation, both the client and the firm should avoid the blame game and focus on correcting the issue and working through the problem. Lastly, I end chapter two by discussing how law firms should communicate overages to their clients. It's not always easy, but both parties to the cost estimate should look to find a middle ground, especially if the work behind the overage was of value to the client.

Operationalizing a successful cost estimate strategy is just as important as the mechanical components that comprise it. In chapter three I share my thoughts around some of the thematic challenges that clients and law firms face when implementing cost estimates. I highlight my experience in a case study where I helped a US insurance company by implementing a cost estimate strategy and provide some guidance for clients looking to do the same. I explore the reasons behind internal corporate resistance that is commonly in some in-house legal departments and companies and how those challenges handicap a successful cost estimate strategy. In this chapter I further address such challenges as lack of executive leadership, in-house counsel apathy, training and support. One of the biggest challenges that I have encountered with regards to the successful implementation of cost estimate strategies has been the inability of lawyers to learn basic accounting skills and familiarize themselves with a process that is valuable to their organizations. Many lawyers still see anything outside of the law, such as administration, not worth their time or that takes away from their ability to bill time. Yet cost estimates are valuable tools by which clients make decisions as to which firm they will engage on any given matter. Resistance to implementing cost estimates does not just reside at firms, but more so in many in-house legal departments or the internal business clients that many in-house legal teams service. Clients are quick to point out that it's not always easy implementing processes that require a little work. All too often people will dismiss something as just another administrative chore. Convincing them otherwise requires work, but it's well worth it once they understand the value and added trust that can be derived through a cost estimate process. I end this chapter with a discussion around trust and how transparency can help achieve that for the client as well as the law firm and a final look at what law firms, not clients, dislike most about cost estimates.

In chapter four, I examine the question of value, specifically how value factors into a cost estimate and how clients can benefit from measuring value using value indicators. Ultimately if a cost estimate has been done well and has outlined the framework for the engagement or the relationship, the client will be satisfied and the firm has delivered value. I provide some insight into how cost estimates provide clients with a strategic advantage and how clients can track the success of a cost estimate. Firms should understand the value of cost estimate data and they should learn to leverage that information for their benefit. Developing a well thought out pricing or cost estimate strategy helps differentiate a firm from its peers and may give it a competitive advantage. Lastly, I tackle the question of whether or not there is still any opportunity to consider subjective or instinctive approaches in today's highly data-driven legal marketplace.

In chapter five, I present my final thoughts around a variety of topics related to cost estimates that clients and firms should be aware of. Many clients are beginning to utilize the cost estimate process and templates and use them as simplified bid processes with multiple firms. I compare the cost estimate process to a more formalized request for proposal (RFP) process and reinforce the belief that firms should approach the cost estimate like an RFP and never assume that they are the only firm that was asked to submit a cost estimate proposal.

If done correctly, a well-defined cost estimate can provide clients with greater visibility and transparency into validating the analysis that is used by a law firm to price its legal services. In chapter five, I also review the importance of trust and how clients should be prepared to challenge a law firm's cost estimate as greater transparency leads to greater comfort for the client and an assurance that the firm is acting in its best interest and that the client understands the value proposition of the cost estimate as it relates to the success of the matter. Those firms that cannot demonstrate how they have objectively determined their cost estimate (and potential cost savings) for the client will be at a competitive disadvantage and increasingly challenged to find newer clients – as existing clients may have moved on to more competitively priced efficient firms.

Finally, I conclude the book with my thoughts on the outlook around the future of cost estimates. Firms that can deliver transparent value through transparent pricing will be able to sustain themselves, satisfy existing clients and be the most attractive to new clients.

# About the author

Richard Brzakala is a recognized legal marketplace thought leader and expert in legal operations, sourcing, and cost efficiency strategies. He has been a trusted advisor to many senior executives and general counsels, having worked and consulted for numerous FIs, law firms, and government agencies. Richard is a frequent speaker, panelist, and writer, having published numerous articles on a variety of legal ops topics such as legal sourcing, winning RFPs, convergence practices, and creating corporate cost-saving strategies. Richard's most recent essay, "The Impact of COVID-19 On Future Legal Operations and the Legal Marketplace", appeared in *Horizon Scanning: Modernizing Legal service Delivery* (ARK Group). He is a contributing author for Thomson Reuters Legal Executive Institute, chairs a number of legal sourcing discussion groups, and also participates in an executive advisory capacity for a global IT legal service company. In 2017, a leading US publication recognized and awarded Richard with its annual Trailblazers award for his work in developing a comprehensive global methodology for evaluating law firm compliance with cyber security standards. Richard is currently working as the global director of external legal services at a large FI in Canada where his mandate includes the oversite of legal ops, compliance, finance, and risk management practices as they relate to the management of external counsel globally.

# Chapter 1:
# The benefits of cost estimates

## Background

Cost estimates are increasing in popularity because many large companies and their internal general counsel are looking for better ways to manage, control, and forecast their external legal costs against internal budget requirements. In this chapter, I explore the value of cost estimates when engaging external counsel, the components that comprise a successful cost plan, and the effects that variances, staffing models, and communication have on the success of a cost estimate.

## The increased popularity of cost estimates

For corporate clients looking to improve how they manage their matters and external legal costs, the implementation of a cost estimate strategy offers clients an excellent opportunity to help achieve those objectives. Since the Great Recession of 2008, many companies that have had to face increased pressures to contain and control their legal spend have turned to all sorts of cost savings, containment, effectiveness, or cost efficiency strategies in the hope that there is something out there that will in some way help them to manage or control escalating legal costs. Consequently, many clients have gone back to the basics and begun focusing greater attention on the service delivery components of their relationships. Value indicators such as communication, staffing, quality of services, deliverables, and timeliness ultimately impact the value a client receives from a law firm. The utilization of cost estimates are also one of those value indicators that are increasing in popularity and importance as many clients realize the integral value a cost estimate strategy brings to a matter or a relationship. Still, many legal operations (legal ops) folks, even law firms, will admit that it's not exactly the sexiest tool (or topic) in today's cost savings arsenal. Ask any lawyer when was the last time they signed up for a course on budgeting or cost estimates and they will probably cringe and say, "I don't remember". Most firms and clients find themselves gravitating more towards such popular topics as alternative fee arrangements (AFAs), legal project management (LPM) practices, knowledge management (KM) or the latest artificial intelligence (AI) tools.

Yet, I believe that cost estimates are a fundamental building block of a matter or a client/law firm relationship. If properly implemented, a cost estimate strategy can afford the client (and the law firm) an opportunity to create a proper foundation that is based on a mutual understanding of expectations, deliverables, pricing, and ultimately the value that is to be delivered from a law firm's work. Its importance to the overall relationship a client enjoys with a law firm should not be underestimated.

Clients utilize cost estimates for a variety of reasons, but perhaps the most common reason is to achieve greater control over costs associated with a matter. Cost estimates offer clients not only a mechanism/tool by which they can control legal costs on a matter but also a framework by which they can define the client's expectations around a matter.

Cost estimates have increased in popularity in large part due to clients looking for ways to improve their understanding of how a law firm prices its work. Clients are looking for greater transparency and comfort around how a law firm calculates the cost for its services. Cost estimate proposals based on visceral or subjective feelings are increasingly frowned upon as many clients have come to expect that a firm will utilize its resources, especially legal ops professionals, to leverage a law firm's historical empirical data in any cost estimate proposal that it proposes to a client. Moreover, clients are also looking for greater accountability and assurances from firms that they will honor their cost estimate proposals.

For years clients have struggled to deal with unexpected law firm overages. I believe clients expect their firms to be accountable and honor any prearranged agreement without any excuses or making unilateral changes without the client's permission. Exceeding a mutually agreed upon cost estimate, without any client notification, has become a cardinal sin as many clients will not tolerate it. There is zero tolerance amongst corporate in-house legal teams with regard to surprise overages, regardless of the depth of the relationship with outside counsel. Failing a solid acceptable explanation on the part of a firm, it should be prepared to write down any unexpected costs that a client finds unacceptable. I believe that the zero tolerance that many clients have in regard to overages is directly attributable to corporate pressures on in-house legal teams and their GC to become more fiscally prudent and responsible for every dollar that is spent on external counsel. All of this has led clients to go back to basics and revisit fundamental approaches, such as the utilization of cost estimates to help them better manage the delivery of legal services. I believe that the fine tuning of anything and everything that can help clients create savings, efficiencies, or predictability in terms of their legal spend and the delivery of legal services is not abating anytime soon.

Sophisticated clients looking to take control of their legal spend have been chasing predictability for many years. AI and automated billing systems have provided clients with a plethora of data that has been both empowering and enriching. Despite the progress in data analytics, clients have still had to rely on firms in order to meet requirements or budget parameters. Cost estimates provide clients not only with greater transparency and predictability, but also a compliance framework from which a law firm is expected to manage a matter. In fact, many clients treat a cost estimate as they would their terms of engagement. Clients have come to consider their cost estimate with a firm to be an extension of their terms of engagement. When issuing cost estimate templates to law firms to complete, clients today will add language to ensure that the law firm understands that their cost estimate proposal, if accepted, becomes a binding price agreement between them and the firm. To that end, clients are expanding on the cost estimate template and including other value added components such as scope definition, instructions around variances and assumptions, delivery of services, staffing ratio, contacts, bid changes etc.

## What do clients look for in a cost estimate?

As the resurgent utilization of cost estimates continues to grow and gain in popularity, many firms will attest to the fact that they encounter many clients that do not have a self-developed cost estimate or budgeting framework to work from. Consequently, law firms servicing such clients may be left with developing a cost estimate strategy or even a basic template that can help the client in understanding a firm's cost proposal.

Cost estimates provided by law firms can vary in detail and complexity and depend on the sophistication of a law firm and even the type of relationship a firm has with its client or the firm's business approach toward clients in general. Ideally, the cost estimate returned to the client should be simple to understand and show clearly the components and calculations used by the firm in determining the cost for its services.

The cost estimate should show the client basic accounting information and quantifiable data of how the firm proposes to staff the matter, listing either specific timekeepers and their respective hourly rates or specific tasks and a fixed price for those tasks.

If hourly rates are used to calculate the cost estimate and those rates are typically discounted for an existing client, then the discounted rates should be used as the benchmark for the cost estimate. It is not uncommon for large firms to mistakenly utilize commercial or street rates, which are typically higher than discounted rates, when calculating cost estimates for their preferred clients. As a best practice, a law firm should validate the rates used as part of its cost estimate process, especially if a client has previously enjoyed the benefit of discounted rates.

For those clients that have embarked on utilizing cost estimates, expectations as to what constitutes a great cost estimate may vary depending on the client's legal and/or business needs as well as their sophistication in how they approach the management of their external law firms. In addition, the frequency of utilization, composition, and complexity of cost estimates that a client utilizes may vary depending on such criteria as risk appetite, practice area, matter scope, timelines, budget, or cost. Each client may differ as to their evolution of law firm management and how they have utilized cost estimates in the past.

Clients with a very low tolerance for risk may require that the firms they hire be extra vigilant and mitigate risk at every opportunity. This consequently impacts how a firm will approach its cost estimate in terms of dealing with variances and assumptions. In such a scenario the clients may want to require that a firm provide them with a strategy or roadmap detailing the scope and all possible variances (the what ifs) in a matter so as to provide the client with as much assurance and confidence that the legal opinion or advice the firm is providing is solid and bullet proof.

This is especially true on matters of significant importance such as extraordinary class actions or defense litigation where there is a high degree of monetary or reputational risk. Capital market acquisitions, high dollar underwriting, and commercial financing transactions are also other practice areas where a client may require an extra high degree of due diligence and detail in the cost estimate that a firm provides to them. Consequently, for those types of scenarios, clients may want to see that the firm provides a greater degree of detail, segregated into tasks or milestones where each task or stage of the matter is clearly defined and priced in the cost estimate so as to provide the client with as much clarity and transparency as is possible.

On highly transactional matters, clients tend to favor flat fee type cost estimates because these types of transactions are typically less complicated, requiring less detail than a significant or extraordinary matter. Nevertheless, on these types of matters, clients look to the firm to identify a fee proposal, such as a flat fee or task based fee, that is easy to manage and provides a comfortable level of detail around the scope. The scope on flat fees, as discussed earlier, doesn't have to be too wordy, but should be sufficient enough to explain the work effort thoroughly.

Many firms favor flat fees as these are one of the easiest cost estimate AFAs for a firm to manage in terms of resources and billing. Clients favor flat fee cost estimates because flat fees are easy to track and monitor and clients do not have to be concerned with tracking multiple professionals working on a matter or concerned about whether or not the matter is staffed appropriately. Under a flat fee cost estimate approach, all of the tasks and the work product that is created for the client are neatly packaged into one item or, in the case of tasks, multiple items with narratives that are very prescriptive with individualized pricing or one final price to cover all of the scope. Details around staff utilization, variance assumptions, or even extended timelines may not be required as the transaction may be very straightforward.

A good example of this can be found in plaintiff litigation – specifically retail collection or residential foreclosure – matters where a firm can submit a cost estimate that proposes to cover all of the costs from the start of a litigation action to obtaining judgement at a flat fee or fixed fee arrangement. From a client's perspective, this type of cost estimate is very straightforward as the judicial procedure is extremely predictable, with very little opportunity for any variances occurring. Moreover, the legal work can be completed by just one professional class or even timekeeper within a specific time frame. Flat fee cost estimates, such as that just described, offer clients an assurance in pricing, procedures, and ultimately the outcome, with little risk to the client. It also allows firms to provide clients with a simplified cost estimate that the client can apply to multiple similar repetitive type matters.

In some circumstances, clients may also require that the firm provide a cost estimate utilizing hourly rates. The best approach for a firm is to make the cost estimate as simple as possible to understand and to monitor. Typically this begins by identifying the scope of the engagement with as much or as little narrative as is required based on the client's requirements. Next, the firm should identify and list all of the timekeepers that will be involved on the matter, their respective hourly rate, their individual professional ranking (associate, partner, clerk etc.), the proposed quantity of time each timekeeper will be expected to work on the matter, and the total cost (fees) that each timekeeper will be expected to bill for the matter. If there are any variances to consider, the firm should exclude these from the scope but include them as separate line items in the cost estimate, along with a narrative explaining how the firm will utilize the variance item.

Some clients may be receptive to firms proposing a blended hourly rate to cover off a specific group of professionals (e.g. all associates will bill a blended rate of $300/hr regardless of year of call) as opposed to individual timekeepers that a firm anticipates it will require to work on a matter. Blended rates offer clients an opportunity to bypass the need to manage staffing models or how professionals are utilized on a client's matter. In the end if blended rate(s) are used, things become a lot easier to manage for both the firm and the client. The tricky part is for clients and firms to find a mutually amenable blended rate that is acceptable to both parties involved in the engagement.

Figure 1 illustrates an hourly rate cost estimate proposal.

| | | | | |
|---|---|---|---|---|
| Definition of scope: | | | | |
| Proposed timekeeper staffing model | | | | |
| Timekeeper name | Class | Hourly rate | Quantity of time | Total cost |
| Jane Smith | Partner | 300 | 4 | 1,200 |
| Alice Ferguson | Associate | 200 | 10 | 2,000 |
| Robert Belinsky | Associate | 250 | 8 | 2,000 |
| Total proposed quantity of time | | | 22 | |
| Total proposed cost (excluding disbursements) | | | | 5,200 |
| Total proposed disbursements | | | | 150 |
| | | | | |
| Potential variances | | | | |
| Variance description | | | | |
| Jane Smith | Partner | 300 | 5 | 1,500 |
| | | | | |
| Total projected variance cost | | | | 1,500 |
| | | | | |
| Total cost of matter (including variances and disbursement costs) | | | | 8,350 |

*Figure 1: Hourly rate cost estimate proposal.*

Regardless of the type of matter or level of complexity, the following components comprise a well thought out and comprehensive cost estimate:

- Scope is defined accurately, definitively and in simple terms;
- A communication plan is included advising which parties are the points of contact on a matter (especially important when dealing with large corporate clients on large transactions in a decentralized legal environment) and the firm's obligations related to such things as variances, overages, conflicts should they arise, anything out of the ordinary should be escalated;

- A timetable is in place setting out delivery dates, expectations, and costs associated with deliverables. These deliverables can be segregated by tasks, hourly rates, or flat fees;
- Proposed pricing is accurate, reasonable, and fair;
- Price/cost is defined and explained, simply and accurately, and most importantly is supported by historical empirical data and not subjective criteria;
- Variances have been accounted for as separate line items, along with a communication plan (i.e. points of contact) should the need arise;
- Staffing plan is included, identifying which timekeeper will be working on the matter, their year of call and professional rank (associate, partner etc.); and
- Disbursement proposal is included as a separate line item, explaining the estimate.

With regard to the proposed price or cost of a matter, firms should expect to be challenged by clients looking for greater assurance and validation in terms of how a firm arrived at their cost proposal. If a firm used information such as historical billing data, timekeeper information, staff utilization ratios, AFA data, profitability forecasting, or predictive modelling or forecasting tools, then the firm should be prepared to share that information with the client. Anything that a firm can do to assure a client that the firm's evaluation and analysis is impartial and fair goes a long way in assuring a client that the cost estimate is thought out and ultimately justifiable. If done properly, the data that a law firm presents to support its cost estimate will speak for itself and the client will recognize that it is reasonable and that they are getting value in the work that the firm proposes to deliver to the client. Delivering a well thought out and comprehensive cost estimate with a logical explanation of how a firm got to its pricing proposal is fundamental to the high expectations that many clients have in today's marketplace.

Despite this, there is always the possibility that there will not be a mutual understanding and agreement on a proposed cost estimate. Firms should be prepared to negotiate, especially if it's in their economic interest or if they have an unwavering commitment to their data. Most clients today expect some level of negotiation when it comes to cost estimates. There is a common expectation that there will be a delta between what the firm proposes in its cost estimate and what the client expects to pay.

Ultimately, it is up to both parties to reach a mutual beneficial agreement. Given all of the changes in the legal marketplace and especially the increased purchasing power (and demand) clients have come to hold, law firms unfortunately are at a disadvantage when it comes to defining what is equitable or fair value. Firms therefore may ultimately be at the mercy of clients in most negotiations as a client can easily walk away in favor of another firm if a client feels that a cost estimate is beyond their budget or if what a firm proposes lacks the value that the client is looking for.

However, there may also be scenarios where a client may provide the firm with a definitive budget or fee cap with an expectation that the firm will meet whatever the fee cap is. The onus in such a scenario rests with the law firm to ensure that the fee cap is economically viable for the firm and that the firm can provide its services to the client without any compromise to quality or value. It may not always be an easy decision for a firm to make as it may have to weigh an unrealistic cost expectation against revenue loss. It's not surprising in a hyper-competitive marketplace where firms may be too quick to accept a client's pricing terms and mandate, only to find themselves later compromised and at an economic disadvantage because the firm had underestimated the work effort or resources required to deliver its services. Compromising quality in exchange for profitability may be an option for some firms, but it is rarely advantageous for a firm in the long run. I have seen clients pay a bill with significant overages, only to never utilize the firm ever again.

Demonstrating a high level of transparency and being proactive are what many clients look to their firms for in the cost estimate process. Firms that can not only answer their clients' requirements, but can also anticipate and proactively provide clients with cost estimate options, stand apart from other firms in a competitive marketplace. What is of tremendous value to a client is the level of openness that a firm can demonstrate and how proactive a firm can be in presenting its cost estimate proposal. Answering as many questions up front in the proposal helps to eliminate the need to negotiate. Clients that agree without any back and forth negotiation or questions recognize that they are comfortable with what the firm has set forth in their cost proposal. All of this, however, is contingent on the client's ability to have defined the scope of the mandate or engagement as clearly and as definitely as possible.

### What don't clients want to see in a cost estimate?

Some time ago I attended a legal trade conference. During an intermission I overheard an exchange between a small group of seasoned in-house counsel lamenting about how the law firms they hire "just don't get it" when it comes to listening and taking direction from the client. "Don't get me wrong – [XYZ] are good lawyers who provide good legal advice, but their service delivery just sucks."

Hardly the best endorsement for a "good" firm, but as I listened on the sidelines it occurred to me that this was neither a revelation nor a one-time occurrence. Three seasoned lawyers went through a very short list of five what I consider to be top law firms, verbally dispatching each one because of their failings when it came to how each firm had repeatedly failed to provide adequate service, listen and communicate properly, or honor their word in regard to proposed cost estimates.

In regard to cost estimates, one lawyer remarked that "it would be nice for them (i.e. the firm) to just once stay within the agreed budget and not surprise me with a ton of work that was unnecessary. I didn't go to law school to fight with a firm over the amount on an invoice." Unfortunately, the discussion, and my eavesdropping, ended abruptly when the conference break ended and we were all summoned back to our conference seats.

The sentiment that one of the in-house lawyers shared, specifically around cost estimates, can probably be understood by many clients who have had similar experiences. The lack of, or suboptimal, client service delivery in the legal industry is not new. What is surprising is the frequency with which client servicing issues continue to reappear despite law firm attempts at trying to train their lawyers on the nuances of service delivery, communication, and listening to clients.

I mentioned earlier how the buyers of legal services are driving the market and demanding a certain level of service delivery and how firms are increasingly being measured against those demands. Given the economic challenges and competitiveness that many firms face in almost all markets, I have found that many firms have begun to pay attention to their clients and have started to make a serious effort to improve how they deal with and service their institutional clients. Firms are finally understanding that not all clients are alike and that a lot of them are not monolithic entities, but diverse organizations requiring special attention, special needs. What may work for one division of a company may not work for another. Firms have started to "clue in" and listen to what their clients are looking for in terms of their individual engagements. Beyond that, firms today are not as tone deaf as they once were in making ubiquitous decisions, such as across the board rate increases or disbursement charges that apply to all clients. This type of myopic behavior is no longer condoned and can end a client/law firm relationship very quickly.

However, despite the progress on service delivery, there continue to be challenges, especially around cost estimates for some firms in understanding what clients need and especially don't want to see in the cost estimates that are proposed to them. The list below is not meant to be exhaustive but it sets out some areas for improvement and what firms should be cognizant of when proposing cost estimates to their clients.

*Assumptions*

If a firm is making assumptions, clearly identify this in the cost estimate as a separate line item to ensure that the client is aware of a potential impact to the overall cost estimate. On large matters I have seen law firms list their assumptions (prescriptively) as a footnote or even addendum to their cost estimate along with a dollar figure next to each assumption. I believe the onus rests on the client to proactively discuss with the firm which assumptions may be required in the course of a matter or which assumption has the greatest potential of being utilized. If a client fails to challenge or question a firm on their assumptions, the firm should approach the client to prompt a discussion.

*Ambiguity*

Cost estimates should be clearly written and definitive. There should not be any ambiguity as it relates to the actual empirical information or data that is being provided to the client. If a task is being used in the cost estimate, the firm should explain clearly and concisely what is expected in completing the task. What confuses and irritates clients is when they see a firm ineffectively or poorly describing a task which later can result in unnecessary cost overages. Some scope statements are purposely drafted to be vague to allow a firm a wide berth to complete additional, often unnecessary, legal work.

*Ignorance*

Apathy and/or ignorance of client expectations is a fatal error for any firm. I stated earlier that lawyers today need to be more aware and better communicators when dealing with clients and that they should never forget that they are in the client service industry. Learning to listen and understand what a client's business needs are is just as important as defining and clarifying scope. Clients will recognize very quickly if a cost estimate is off its mark and the firm has disregarded their requirements. The firm will have to validate why they chose the proposal they did. In other words, the firm will have to back up its proposal with either real data (historical experience, costs or outcomes) or a legal basis (historical legal precedents or experience). Anything short of that will not fly with business-savvy clients. An example of this can be where a client has been adamant and insisted that there not be any assumptions calculated into the overall cost estimate. However, after its due diligence and analysis, the firm believes that there needs to be some sort of contingency to protect the client. Adding the cost for assumptions (as a separate line item) is fine, even if the client did not request any assumptions. Things like assumptions can be explained as pre-emptive scenarios aimed at mitigating risk for the client.

*Undefined scope*

Poorly defined scope is probably one of the biggest challenges facing firms, as well as clients. As already discussed, defining scope requirements is considered to be the most important component of the cost estimate. Firms are at less risk of encountering issues with their clients on highly transactional or commoditized legal work where defining the tasks or objectives of a matter are pretty straightforward. It is on more complex legal matters that both the client and firm share a mutual responsibility to review and agree on the final description of scope. Unfortunately, many times the client is too busy or difficult to contact and the firm, for whatever reason, may decide to make some assumption on defining the scope on their own. This is a risky approach and may backfire for the firm. In such circumstances there is always the potential that the scope may have failed to represent the business needs of the client, the scope was incomplete, or perhaps conflicted with another business requirement that the firm was not made aware of. Firms should always seek proper clarification and written instructions when defining the scope of a matter.

*Estimates*

Price range cost estimates are increasingly frowned upon and resisted by many sophisticated clients, but some firms continue to utilize them. When compared to other approaches, clients view price range estimates as a somewhat casual, even inaccurate, approach to presenting a cost information. Price range estimates typically propose a dollar range estimate for a task or significant piece of legal work. The dollar range for the task may or may not be significant and will include some type of task description for the work that is expected to be completed for that dollar range. The total price for the firm's legal services is not definitive but instead presented in the form of a price range (e.g. $5,000 to $25,000). The client does not have a precise expectation of what they will pay for the final legal work product, but at least know that the firm will be expected to be within the proposed price range.

My experience with price range estimates has been less than optimal as many firms have typically charged clients at the higher end of the price range and in some instances presented a huge delta between the low end and high end of a range. Moreover, price ranges on cost estimates don't afford the client any real opportunity to guarantee a specific price or even that the legal services to be delivered will be billed at the lower end of the price range.

Many clients today are skeptical when it comes to price ranges, realizing that they are not meaningful in terms of reliability and question a law firm's motives for even proposing such an arrangement that seems to be skewed in favor of the firm for profitability reasons. Clients have come to believe that the firm is incentivized to almost always bill out their time at the higher end of the range, which puts the client at a significant disadvantage. Most clients typically don't expect to pay the high end of the range, so inevitably there is almost always a discussion about lowering the cost from a dissatisfied client who thinks they have been overcharged. In addition, price ranges don't afford clients the same level of transparency as other types of cost estimates. More and more clients are increasingly looking to the firms that they hire to provide them with definitive cost expectations and not a price range with a very wide delta. In short, firms that propose price range estimates risk sending the wrong message to potential clients and create a competitive disadvantage for themselves as well as a potentially uncomfortable discussion with their clients should the client question a bill.

#### *Overstaffing*

Overstaffing has been an issue for many clients who want to see firms utilizing only those resources that are absolutely necessary. Gone are the days when firms can staff up a matter with any professional they like on to a client's matter. Firms today know that clients have the ability to analyze staffing patterns to determine the staffing ratio at a firm and whether the firm is utilizing the best and most experienced professionals on the matter. Ultimately, it is the client that makes a determination as to whether they received value for the cost of the professionals working on the matter.

Clients are increasingly looking to have specific (experienced) professionals work on their matters. Perhaps there is a lawyer at a firm that is exceptionally knowledgeable or experienced in dealing with specific areas of the law or has worked on other matters for other companies that the client is aware of. Typically, clients will want the most experienced professional working on their matter and look less favorably on firms that seem to staff matters with many junior associates that the client may see as adding very little value.

Before adding any professional or timekeeper to a cost estimate proposal, a firm should consider the potential contribution of the professional to the matter. In the past, firms would typically over-staff their matters so as to ensure that they mitigated any and all potential risk that related to a client's matter. Inevitably, this type of strategy often resulted in overages and frequent discussions with disgruntled clients. Firms got a bad reputation for over-billing for unnecessary work.

Given that many experienced law firms today have the benefit of automated precedents and legal knowledge capital at their fingertips, firms are expected to know – with a high degree of certainty – what to expect in terms of workload, resourcing, and costs on many commoditized and transactional matters. Even on complicated matters, firms today have the ability to predict staffing models for specific milestone events or tasks.

All this to say, clients have come to expect that when firms bid on potential work through an RFP process or when they submit a cost estimate proposal, that they have a higher degree of accuracy, based on empirical historical data and legal knowledge when it comes to staffing their matters, and that the client gets the benefit of that information in the cost estimate that a firm proposes. Consequently, this knowledge should be reflective in the cost estimate that a firm proposes to a client. If junior associates are needed, then perhaps reiterating to the client that they will be managed closely by the partners and their time will be reviewed and assessed before the client is billed will provide some level of assurance to the client that the firm is serious about managing its staff on the client's matter. When assessing a firm's staffing proposal, clients are looking for firms to identify the specific professional by name, year of call, geographic location, and practice group expertise. Not too long ago, firms had absolute control and discretion to manage and staff a client's matter with whomever they liked.

When it comes to the staffing component in a cost estimate, firms should be prepared to explain how they came up with their staffing strategy. Some clients may in fact insist in their cost estimate that specific professionals be utilized or not utilized due to previous poor performance, lack of expertise and/or experience, or the client finds them too expensive. Firms may also have based a large component of their cost estimate on certain professionals working a matter. If the client disagrees with the firm's staffing ratio or whom they think should be utilized, firms should be prepared to revise the cost estimate significantly.

### *Expenses*

Another area of concern for most clients is seeing high estimates for disbursements and expenses as part of a firm's cost estimate. These will typically appear as a separate line item towards the end of a cost estimate, unless the firm states clearly that it has excluded disbursements from its cost proposal. Whether disbursements are included or not, the client should be made aware of what to expect, even if the firm thinks the total cost of disbursements is expected to be a nominal amount. However, if high estimates are provided by the firm, then again, these should be supported with some level of description to help provide an assurance to the client that the disbursement costs are necessary and justified. All of this speaks to a greater level of responsibility on the part of the firm to provide excellent client service by making legal costs more transparent for the client.

Lastly, cost estimates that propose potential ancillary costs related to the hiring of additional third party law firms or for managing co-counsel on a client's matter should be discussed in advance of any formal cost estimate that is submitted to a client. I have seen law firms include line items for the management of third party service providers and co-counsel on their cost estimates. These line items tend to appear as proposed management, consultant, or third party type fees to be potentially billed by the law firm to a client for "overseeing" and "managing" (usually) co-counsel on a matter. For many clients who have direct relationships with their panel firms, this is a non-starter and unpalatable as clients expect their panel firms to manage any third parties on their own, absorbing any ancillary costs, as administrative overhead. Different clients have differing views on third party costs and how they should be treated. If a client has a complicated matter that will require offshore counsel and a firm to manage that type of relationship, then perhaps there is an opportunity to include those types of costs in the client's cost estimate. Having a discussion with the client in advance of submitting a cost proposal is always the best approach.

## How clients are empowered by cost estimates

Business groups within large corporate environments that are accountable for their legal spend have for years struggled to accurately project or forecast legal resource costs or project expenditures on legal budgets. Although not a panacea for all legal forecasting challenges, clients who can learn to leverage and analyze their historical billing patterns and cost estimate data may be in a position to resolve their forecasting challenges. Cost estimate data may be used to make better informed, accurate decisions and financial projections. Historical data can also help clients identify preferred law firms or match up law firm expertise with business needs and budget requirements without having to utilize lengthy and protracted requests for proposal or competitive bid processes.

Clients are always looking to fine tune their panel of firms or perhaps to rationalize an already large and extensive list of providers. Utilizing cost estimate data allows clients to conduct cross-firm comparisons to identify firms that will yield the greatest cost benefit and savings for the client.

The engagement process with new and even existing firms is another area of benefit for clients looking to leverage cost estimate data as the assignment of matters can be expedited to firms where a client has already agreed to a pricing arrangement that is based on reliable and trustworthy information, thereby eliminating the need for any unnecessary engagement negotiations around pricing.

In the case of large litigation matters, cost estimate data can be used to build out budgets related to milestone tasks or even to identify settlement opportunities (sooner rather than later). Many clients today utilize a combination of their proprietary cost estimate and legal spend data coupled to forecasting software to assist them in designing probability models to better assist them with their settlement strategies.

The value of cost estimate data, or any legal spend data for that matter, cannot be understated and should not be ignored. The analysis of cost estimate data brings with it a discipline in thinking and decision making that has traditionally not existed in the legal marketplace until fairly recently. Leveraging any type of historical spend data or budget data allows the information to "speak" to the client and guide them in their decision making process.

There is a greater uniformity of thought amongst progressive law departments that spend data is empowering for not only the client but for firms that strive and invest in being extremely cost competitive and efficient. In the end, regardless of how great the data, the data does not make the decisions. The data allows clients to be empowered to make better decisions and guides the client to make the right decision or find the most cost competitive or efficient firm. Therefore, it is also important to understand a bit about the mechanics, technology, and the processes clients leverage in tracking cost estimate data. In other words, how do they do it.

## The benefits of cost estimates to a law firm

Years ago, when I started to manage firms, I had a meeting with a securities lawyer in New York and I asked him how he came up with his cost estimate. I'll never forget his answer. The lawyer leaned forward across a large onyx table that separated us, lowered his voice almost to a whisper and said, "Son, it's coming from inside of here [pointing to his chest] and here [pointed at his forehead], and 31 years of experience". He finished by stating, "...and I am never wrong". I got back to my office and repeated the discussion I had with an executive in my legal department at the time. The executive was stunned, thinking that the estimate we had received earlier from the lawyer was backed up by real empirical information. Moreover, the executive was about to recommend the lawyer's estimate to be accepted by the company's board of directors. He promptly instructed me to never use the lawyer or his firm again. Thankfully, most firms today have moved away from subjective cost estimates as sophisticated clients will no longer tolerate standalone, subjective methodologies as the basis for cost estimates, but instead are requiring cost estimates backed up by real empirical historical or market data.

Expectations in today's marketplace and going forward are that firms should be in a position to provide greater granularity and clarity in the pricing information they present to clients and not just simply rely on a subjective and intuitive approach such as my experience with the lawyer in New York. The intuitive approach for many clients has become unpalatable and unacceptable.

I see tremendous benefit and value for those firms who utilize cost estimate strategies. Clients appreciate the extra level of transparency, backed up by real data, as synonymous with honesty and trust – two precious characteristics that, in the eyes of many clients, firms have struggled to achieve and portray.

As clients continue to ask for more and continue to raise their service expectations, firms should expect to be challenged, if they haven't already, by clients who want a higher level of validation. Sure, this might mean extra work for a firm, but I think it's worth it for both the client and the firm.

Firms looking to increase their competitiveness or join a client's panel need to distinguish themselves from their peers. Developing a cost estimate strategy to help clients is an opportunity that is often overlooked or underestimated in terms of value by some firms. Instead, all firms, whether on a panel or not, need to appreciate what their clients value and not become reticent in their relationships.

Clients welcome a proactive approach, especially if they didn't ask for it and recognize that what the firm is proposing has merit and can add value to their organization.

Firms that understand that it is no longer just about the practice of law and legal advice, but is also about the business of law and meeting client expectations around how they want to be serviced, will enjoy a market advantage over their peers. Providing a well thought out cost estimate demonstrates a firm's commitment to honesty, transparency, strategic thinking, efficiency, and a dedication to service delivery.

This is especially true in today's legal marketplace, which has become increasingly homogenized where many firms look alike, are doing the same things, offering the same services at the same price. Cost estimates offer firms a fundamental yet excellent opportunity at distinguishing themselves from others while also profiling a firm's value proposition. If a firm can learn how to leverage the right internal resources, create processes around data analysis, and ultimately package their information into a standardized framework that is straightforward, transparent, and easy for a client to understand, they will stand out amongst their peers and improve their profitability.

The hyper-competitiveness is not abating anytime soon. Cost estimates are a basic fundamental framework that are underutilized, yet integral to almost every matter from a pricing perspective. They are by no means a panacea for all the challenges that clients face but, if done right, a good cost estimate strategy can help a law firm build greater client loyalty, retention, and ultimately profits.

# Chapter 2:
# The mechanics of cost estimates

As firms increasingly have to comply with a multitude of operational requirements for different clients in different industries, they are starting to turn to their information technology and data management systems – such as internal accounting software or document management systems for historical billing data – to help them determine cost estimates. Technology and e-billing tools have come a long way in the past decade, so much so that many firms today have the capability of slicing and dicing historical billing data to help themselves better understand the best pricing options for both themselves and their clients in terms of what is reasonable yet still profitable for the firm. Those options can vary from the hourly rate billing model to various AFAs and value priced considerations.

## The continued utilization of the hourly rate billing model

Over the years there has been a lot written about the anticipated demise of the hourly rate billing model. Many clients recognize that billing for legal services on the basis of hourly rates is nothing more than an incentive for a firm to bill more time and be rewarded to be inefficient. Proponents of AFAs have argued for years that the utilization of hourly rates only rewards a law firm for the quantity of time it bills a client and not necessarily the results. In short, many proponents of AFAs believe that the hourly rate model rewards and incentivizes inefficiency.

For law firms it has not been easy to move away from a business model that it has used for the past 60 years to generate profits. Most firms compensate their lawyers using formulas that rely heavily on the quantity of time they bill their clients. Finding alternative billing models to replace hourly billing has been a challenge and almost all firms continue to leverage hourly rates in many of the cost estimates they provide their clients.

Clients, on the other hand, want any pricing option that can demonstrate savings for them. They have been attracted to AFAs but, as many will attest, there is work to be done to ensure that they are receiving cost savings. This asymmetrical balance of clients wanting to pay less and utilize something other than hourly rates is juxtaposed by firms married to a profit model where lawyers are incentivized to bill more. While there has been an active movement with many clients to move away from the hourly rate model and embrace alternative and value based billing models, the change in pricing philosophy has not totally stopped firms and clients from continuing to utilize hourly rates, especially in regard to cost estimates.

Clients as well as firms continue to utilize hourly rates in a variety of practice areas and scenarios including most matters where cost estimates are required. One can make the argument that perhaps this is not the best approach to achieve value, but as many clients will attest, it is perhaps the easiest approach for the client and the firm to mutually arrive at a fair price for the legal services. In the end, cost estimate calculations using the hourly rate model are easy to calculate and understand in terms of determining profitability for a firm and value for the client.

## Cost estimates based on task-based billing models

If a law firm is providing a cost estimate for specific tasks or significant legal milestones, the firm should be able to quantify how much time (i.e. number of hours) and the total cost it expects to charge for each of the tasks.

Typically, task-based cost estimates should include a staffing model to identify which law firm timekeepers will be assigned to the matter, the quantity of time each timekeeper will be expected to contribute, and the total cost quantified in terms of dollars for each of the timekeepers assigned to the task. If the scope of the engagement has been defined properly, all of these cost items will allow the client to see the math behind the firm's value or cost proposal.

If task-based billing is being proposed by a firm as part of their cost estimate, the firm should be aware that many clients today view task based billing as an alternative fee arrangement (AFA) to the traditional hourly rate billing model and consequently expect to see value (i.e. cost savings) in the work that a law firm delivers to them. In these types of scenarios, clients typically are only focused on the firm completing the task on time and on budget. Because of this, firms may be tempted to view task-based billing in the simplest terms, focusing squarely on how they can expend the least costly resources to get the task completed and still maintain their profit margins. This type of perspective may become problematic for both the client and the firm if the work product is less than optimal. Thankfully, most reputable firms today, regardless of the AFA, ensure that their matters are staffed properly so as to deliver excellent legal services.

### Utilizing dollar ranges in cost estimate proposals

Dollar range cost estimates that provide the client with a proposed range (e.g. $5,000 – $10,000) for a law firm's services have been a traditional favorite used by many firms. However, sophisticated clients are increasingly moving away from dollar ranges as they provide less than an accurate approach to defining the cost of a matter and incentivize a firm to bill for their services at the maximum of the dollar range. With all their drawbacks and a common disdain amongst corporate clients, why is it that they continue to be utilized?

I believe the answer can be explained firstly by a fundamental failing on the part of many clients to define matter scope or business requirements accurately, which compels the firm to make assumptions and allowances that inevitably result in a price range as opposed to a definitive task cost or flat fee proposal. This is especially true if there has not been any follow up discussion with the client to clarify scope or to more accurately define the parameters of the engagement so as to remove as much ambiguity as possible. If the firm has reached out and the client's efforts to define scope have been less than optimal, the firm is left with no other option than to default to a dollar range in its cost estimate proposal. In such a scenario, clients should give extra leniency and consideration to a firm's proposal and to understanding the basis on which the firm proposed its cost estimate. Therefore, as much as clients want and expect definitive cost estimates, they may not always be readily available and the onus therefore rests squarely on the firm to explain to their clients the basis for the firm's approach and why they chose to provide a dollar range to the client. Without a logical explanation the firm risks the client making false assumptions that may have an adverse impact on the firm's engagement.

Secondly, firms tend to gravitate to price range estimates because of the nature of the matter. For matters that are not routine or transactional in nature, firms may struggle to definitively provide an accurate cost estimate because of things that are simply beyond the firm's control. Matters may have a multitude of complicating issues, uncertainties around strategy, variances, or finally a multitude of probable scenarios that may or may not take place and that the client and the firm may not definitively expect to take place.

In this second scenario, firms and clients may not be able to define a strategy and a definitive cost estimate at the outset of an engagement because of a multitude of factors. For example, on complicated litigation matters with multiple parties or on complicated commercial contract matters involving intense multi-party negotiations, a variety of unexpected issues may arise at any time during the course of a matter. Going into those types of matters, firms can expect the unexpected to occur at any time. Putting a fixed cost in place in such scenarios is both impractical and unrealistic.

All of this presents an enormous challenge for firms to define costs at the outset of a matter. Many firms continue to struggle with highly complicated matters and are uncomfortable with nailing down fixed fees or providing clients with flat fees when there is a multitude of variances or the matter is highly unpredictable. Still, advances in data analytics and forecasting software have allowed some firms to gain an advantage over others as they have mastered data analytics and learned how to utilize their historical data in complex litigation matters – such as where they have learned to help their clients forecast various settlement scenarios and the legal costs associated with those scenarios. Many times those types of legal costs are presented to defendants in litigation as a dollar range scenario for specific stages of an action. Including settlement projection strategies along with cost estimates can be a significant market advantage for firms.

Given the many variables and uncertainties in some types of legal matters, it is understandable why a firm would select a dollar range estimate as its preferred and most realistic pricing option for its client. In these types of scenarios, dollar ranges are acceptable, but again the onus rests on the firm to update the client as to the status of its work effort and its billable time in relation to the dollar range agreed upon with the client.

For example, if a dollar range of $150k to $250k has been mutually agreed upon, the firm should proactively provide the client with regular updates (in increments of $25,000) as to how much work and time billed as it relates to the dollar range. This type of communication helps mitigate against overage surprises and allows all parties to recalibrate should a strategy and its associated costs exceed original expectations.

Unless clients specifically request a firm not to utilize dollar ranges in their cost estimates, firms should consider the utilization of dollar ranges, provided the following criteria have been met:

- All other pricing options and AFAs have been considered and a determination has been made that they are not practical and have been eliminated from consideration;

- The matter is complicated and has a high degree of assumptions occurring; and
- The client has failed to provide adequate descriptions around scope.

If a firm is going to present a dollar range estimate as part of its cost estimate proposal, consideration should be given to include the following elements in order that the dollar range is acceptable and of value to the client:

- The delta in the dollar range should not be greater than 40 percent (e.g. 5k–6k);
- A detailed narrative accompanies the dollar range parameter to help the client understand the work effort and the cost of any assumptions;
- A cost break down of additional assumptions accompanied by a narrative explaining the logic behind the assumption;
- A communication plan (similar to other cost estimates) be included to assist the client, and law firm, in understanding clear expectations, goals, timelines, points of contact and deliverables;
- A notification plan to revisit the dollar range when a law firm's work effort has reached 50 percent of the maximum threshold of the dollar range;
- Detailed narrative around specific caveats should they be needed if the dollar range is exceeded;
- Details of how any other pricing arrangements or AFAs will be utilized, should the need arise; and
- Details specific to how disbursements will be billed to the client, should the need arise.

Lastly, clients need to be cognizant that any dollar ranges that are presented may also have a built in assumption cushion. In order to be assured that a firm is delivering the right dollar range, the firm should be prepared to explain how it arrived at the cost estimate, any historical basis for the dollar range, and whether or not any assumptions have been priced into the dollar range. If the firm does not, or worse cannot, provide additional information to the client around how it arrived at its dollar range, the firm runs the risk of being challenged by a highly skeptical client, or worse yet the firm may stand to lose the engagement because of its inability to be transparent in defining its methodology. When there is a lack of transparency, there is a lack of assurance, which ultimately impacts trust. Clients who cannot trust a firm will in all likelihood stop using the firm.

### Buyer beware – stay away from commercial (street) rates in cost estimates

Firms have for years been utilizing a combination of pricing arrangements for different clients. None of these arrangements has been more controversial than what the legal market refers to as "street" or "commercial" rates and are also referred to as "rack rates". Commercial rates are typically higher than any other hourly rate a firm uses to bill its professionals' time.

Law firms contend that commercial rates are established by empirical market forces and variables, analysis and a variety of other economic criteria such as administrative overhead, experiential factors, market GDP, and the firm's own market intelligence and competitiveness analysis.

Preferred clients, typically those who designate their firms on panels or as designated counsel status, usually get the benefit of some sort of discount off commercial rates by the law firm in exchange for the firm being on the client's panel. Most clients expect that discounted rates will be utilized if the firm uses an hourly rate in its cost estimate proposal.

Firms have for years maintained that commercial rates are the standard by which the "street" or market has established the true value of a professional's time. Consequently, when firms offer their clients hourly rate discounts, the firms typically benchmark their discounts against the commercial (higher) rate.

What has become controversial in today's marketplace is the belief amongst corporate clients that commercial rates are nothing more than an optical illusion supported by the legal industry to provide unwitting clients with the illusion of cost savings. Commercial rates are used more often than not for benchmarking purposes and for the benefit of larger clients to provide them with the appearance of a discount by not charging the client a higher (inflated) rate.

Commercial rates would be similar to the mark-up pricing that occurs in other retail industries. A good example is the auto industry where car dealerships mark up the price of a car by 100 percent and then offer a whopping 30 percent discount tomorrow off the car sticker price. Buyers are attracted to purchasing the vehicle, thinking they are getting a great deal by saving 30 percent when in fact it's the opposite and the dealer is in fact pocketing a 70 percent mark-up/profit. Moreover, as many more clients challenge the efficiency and value of the hourly rate model, suspicion has grown around the commercial rate methodology as being nothing more than a preeminent form of manufacturing profit margins on the basis of unwitting and unsophisticated clients.

Fortunately, sophisticated clients no longer allow their panel firms to benchmark cost savings against commercial street rates. Clients are increasingly challenging firms on their tabulation methodology to understand and confirm whether or not commercial rates have been used in the firm's calculations and as part of their cost estimate proposal.

Despite a ubiquitous disdain amongst corporate clients in regard to commercial rates I have repeatedly seen firms utilizing their commercial rates as the basis for their clients' cost estimates. From a client's perspective, it's surprising, in fact shocking, to see that the practice of benchmarking cost savings against commercial rates continues to be prevalent in the marketplace.

Clients expect far more from firms today than ever before, especially those firms looking to make new inroads with new prospective clients. To better align their interests with those of their clients, firms should improve their awareness around what clients expect in terms of pricing and how they expect their firms to calculate their cost estimate proposals. Commercial rates are an excellent example of how clients today have been empowered by data to challenge traditional law firm practices in order to better understand how cost differentials impact cost estimates that are proposed by law firms.

## Leveraging historical data and work

I believe that clients have a higher expectation from their panel firms and consequently there is an extra onus of responsibility on the firms to ensure that the cost estimates that they deliver are accurate, competitive, and transparent. Regardless of the size of the client, market, or industry, all clients are looking to benefit from the transparency and predictability that a cost estimate offers them and that the cost estimate proposal they receive is based on sound empirical (historical) data. There is a growing expectation in the marketplace for firms to work more efficiently and effectively and, whenever possible, leverage historical knowledge and data for the benefit of the client.

In recent years there has been a lot of discussion about how law firms are increasingly attracted to the utilization of automation and AI to "recycle" their opinions and the legal knowledge that exists within a firm's document and matter management systems. I have personally heard a lot from firms on this topic as well, but unfortunately very few firms have actually committed enough meaningful capital or demonstrated a firm-wide move in this direction worthy enough of making a significant impact on either their clients or the marketplace. Moving the profit pendulum away from what can only be characterized as an industry-wide addiction to the hourly rate profit model is no easy task. But clients are increasingly demanding it and looking for innovative and smart cost estimate proposals that are focused on the value that can be derived from historical information, opinions, and precedents, rather than reinventing the wheel on every new engagement.

However, there continues to be a huge lag in so far as adopting to these types of cost saving opportunities. Clients will scrutinize proposed cost estimates and ask how a firm came up with the whole or part of the cost estimate, especially if the cost estimate is greater than what a client has been paying historically. In other words, clients are increasingly growing tired of paying more, each year, for the same type of work that a firm has been doing for years. Clients don't mind paying for legal work, provided they feel they are getting value for that work and that the effort that went into that work is justified. If a client knows that a firm works efficiently internally, the cost that is tied to the work product is unlikely to be an issue provided the quality of the legal work is what the client expected. Cost or price only becomes an issue in the absence of value or if the quality of the legal work is suboptimal.

When a panel firm has acted for a client on historical matters, similar in scope, it is not unreasonable for a client to expect that a firm reduce its cost estimate given that the firm (i) has historical familiarity with the engagement, (ii) has the ability to recycle its previous (historical) work product, and (iii) expects to expend fewer resources at a reduced quantity of time for the benefit of the client.

Nothing would impress an existing or potential client more than if a firm proposed a cost estimate that was extremely competitive but also supported by a firm-wide efficiency program that focused on driving client costs down without compromising either the service or work product.

## Highlighting cost savings and efficiency in a cost estimate

The data that a cost estimate is comprised of is critical to the matter. However, firms should also consider including a cost efficiency line item or "cost savings" item as part of their cost estimate proposal. Highlighting how a firm can potentially save a client money is important information and should not be overlooked or minimized when a firm proposes a cost estimate.

Traditionally, firms have not been the best at communicating this strategy to their clients as it has been a challenge historically for many firms to simply justify their market pricing in the face of highly skeptical and biased clients. In fact, I would go so far as to say that many firms probably never thought of, or saw a need, to create internal efficiencies to stay off having to increase their hourly rates at the beginning of every calendar year. Historically, it has been easier to just raise rates, rather than look inwards for efficiencies and savings. The market has changed this practice as many clients look down on unjustified automatic increases as a sense of entitlement that is not well received and in many circumstances challenged by fiscally prudent clients.

Many firms who have clung to the traditional hourly rate model have tried to impress their clients by letting them know that their firm is charging them a "preferred" or "discounted" rate – discounted of course from artificially high "street" rates or commercial rates that are typically 40 percent more than what the firm would charge most of its clients. Sophisticated clients today have increasingly become skeptical of firms that try to demonstrate cost savings by using the street rate benchmarking approach. Clients recognize that it is nothing more than an illusion of purported savings that are not real. Clients are increasingly attracted to firms that can demonstrate true cost savings that are beyond the benchmarking approach. Firms looking to make an impact with their cost estimate proposal should highlight how their internal business processes, KM, or LPM practices or latest technology software improvements (e.g. consolidating and recycling historical client info, precedents, briefs, precedents etc.) will help them deliver excellent advice more expediently and efficiently for the benefit of the client. If all of this can be translated into a cost savings dollar figure for the client to see, what better way is there for a firm to capture the attention (and business) of a potential client?

## The importance of understanding variances and assumptions

When there is a need for a law firm to make assumptions in the course of a matter, clients should insist on having those assumptions accounted for in the scope of their cost estimate. If a firm is unable to quantify an exact dollar amount around a specific assumption or variance, then at the very least the assumption should be clearly described and documented to serve as advance notification to the client of a potential impact to the overall cost estimate.

Both the client and the firm should also understand and agree upon the circumstances that would permit a firm to act on an assumption and whether or not the firm needs to pre-clear any additional work (related to the assumption) with the client or whether the firm can proceed unilaterally, exercising its own discretion, provided certain conditions, tasks, or triggers during the scope are met.

## Calculating the variance cushion

Many clients are unaware that firms typically build into their cost estimates what I like to refer to as the "variance cushion". The variance cushion is an additional cost that the firm has calculated, over and above the actual scope of engagement, to account for any unforeseen variances or assumptions that may affect a firm's cost estimate. If faced with unexpected variances, firms typically will be required to deploy additional resources and extra time to work on an unforeseen issue, task or something that was not scoped in the original engagement instructions or may have surfaced during the course of the matter that the firm believes is material to the matter. Clients may be surprised to learn that a variance cushion may account for as much as 20 percent or more of the original cost estimate.

The variance cushion allows the firm to take advantage of billing for additional work should it need to without having to ask the client for permission to increase the original cost estimate. While some cynics would argue that it is simply a profitability tool that a firm includes to bolster its revenue stream, others see it as a necessary element that serves both parties well by eliminating the time and resources required to otherwise renegotiate a cost estimate if the variance cushion was excluded from the original cost estimate.

From a client's perspective, it is important to ask the firm what percentage of its cost estimate is attributable to the variance cushion or assumptions. If the scope of the engagement is definitive and does not require assumptions to be built into it, then it is reasonable for a client to ask that the firm remove the variance cushion and lower the firm's cost estimate.

I believe the onus rests on the client to determine whether the scope of the engagement or the task merits a variance cushion. Clients in different industries will require different levels of operational risk to function and self-regulate. Ultimately, a client's risk appetite determines the level of risk (i.e. risk posture) that is acceptable. It is this risk posture, of what is and isn't acceptable, that ultimately determines the level of due diligence (i.e. law firm legal work plus time and resources) that is required on a matter. The onus rests squarely on the client to determine and provide guidance to the firm as to whether or not a variance cushion should be included in a matter.

Increasingly, I am finding that many corporate clients want to see the variance cushion priced outside of the firm's cost estimate and are increasingly putting caveats and price caps on how variance cushions can be utilized should the need arise. This approach is probably the most amicable and fair to both parties.

An example of a cost estimate template that can be provided to a law firm is highlighted in Figure 2.

**Law firm cost estimate summary - including variance**

| Matter scope | | |
|---|---|---|
| **Matter phase description - major milestones** | **Total estimated hours** | **Total fees** |
| Preparation and registration of standard security documentation (e.g. General Security Agreement, moveable hypothecs, insurance assignments, investment property pledge agreements, securities account control agreements) | 7 | 3,050 |
| **TOTAL** | **7** | **3,050** |

| Staffing model/team - partners, associates, others | | | | |
|---|---|---|---|---|
| **Name of professional** | **Professional ranking** | **Hourly rate** | **Total hours to be billed** | **Total fees** |
| John Smith | Partner | 540 | 5 | 2,700 |
| Jane Sykorski | Associate | 225 | 1 | 225 |
| Edith Bench | Other (clerk) | 125 | 1 | 125 |
| **TOTAL** | | | **7** | **3,050** |

| Staffing summary | | |
|---|---|---|
| **Professional ranking** | **Total hours** | **Total fees** |
| Partner | 5 | 2,700 |
| Associate | 1 | 225 |
| Other professionals | 1 | 125 |
| **TOTAL** | **7** | **3,050** |

| Variances/assumptions - IF REQUIRED - additional cost | | | | |
|---|---|---|---|---|
| Additional scope - variances: negotiation if necessary (estimated cost) | | | | |
| **Name of professional** | **Professional ranking** | **Hourly rate** | **Total hours to be billed** | **Additional total fees** |
| John Smith | Partner | 540 | 3 | **1,620** |

*Figure 2: Law firm cost estimate summary.*

## Leveraging law firm resources to develop cost estimates

The data component in a cost estimate is critically important, but just as important is understanding how firms go about formulating their cost estimate and what resources they utilize to assist them in their processes of formulating a cost estimate. Firms vary in their procedures and the data they use to determine cost estimates for their clients. Different data professionals may be used to determine different parts of a cost estimate for a client. It's not uncommon to find several different professionals working on a cost estimate at any given time.

For example, project managers, marketing specialists, data analysts, and finance, e-billing, and accounting specialists, in addition to lawyers, clerks, and even knowledge management professionals, may be individually or collectively tapped to participate in developing a cost estimate for a client. As previously mentioned, the empirical data used in formulating a cost estimate is critically important, but so too are the subjective, non-quantifiable factors such as professional knowledge, practice group and business group experience, non-lawyer relationships, even experiences with other differing clients, can all come into play and be leveraged in strategizing a proposal for an existing or new client. This may sound contradictive to what I stated earlier where clients are looking for non-subjectively based cost estimates; however, in this scenario of strategizing a cost estimate for a new or existing client, all elements, including non-empirical elements, can be leveraged to ensure that the cost estimate is customized for the needs of a specific client, especially if the cost estimate is unique or exceptionally complicated. Relying on simply empirical data may not be sufficient or adequate to meet the client's needs.

In addition to the data professionals, there may be a need to involve another group of legal professionals who are mostly comprised of managing partners, practice group leaders and/or relationship partners, who may have intimate historical experience and business knowledge of an existing client or expertise in a specific area or exposure to specific industry groups in the case of new potential clients.

Legal professionals are important to any cost estimate exercise as they can add value by sharing anecdotal information that may not be empirical in nature, but is nevertheless relevant to the cost estimate process and/or final proposal. Legal professionals can add value to the cost estimate by:

- Sharing intimate knowledge of a client's business model;
- Understanding a client's current and future business strategy;
- Identifying a client's risk appetite;
- Identifying nuances around how the client manages their matters;
- Understanding the overall client history and current state of affairs; and
- Identifying the firm's past performance on other matters, rate of success on other cost estimates or sharing market knowledge from other client experiences on similar matters.

Whether it's the data professionals or legal professionals at a firm who produce the final cost estimate, there is a certain level of expectation that whatever numbers are included in the cost estimate, they are always negotiable should the client require some flexibility.

## Calculating the staffing utilization ratio

As part of the cost estimate process, firms should be reminded to staff a matter appropriately to ensure that there is, at the very least, an equitable distribution of work among all professional classes, especially non-partner classes. With an abundance of billing data available to corporate clients, billing data can be mined to understand and gain greater visibility into how a law firm staffs its matters. I refer to this data analysis process as the law firm staffing utilization ratio, whereby different legal professional classes are measured against each other in terms of the quantity of time, hourly rate, or even tasks they have completed in regard to a specific matter, practice area, or their total historical billing over a specific period of time. Ideally, for many cost-conscious clients, legal work on transactional type matters should flow from high- to low-priced legal classes (e.g. from partners to associates or other classes) whenever possible.

Clients have come to realize that how a firm staffs its matters plays a significant part in the economics of a matter. Firms are increasingly being asked to propose staffing models that require mid-level timekeepers (usually mid-level associates) to do greater quantities of work away from higher-priced partners. This requirement is especially important on uncomplicated matters that require less seasoned legal expertise.

For many cost-conscious legal departments, law firm staffing utilization ratios have been used as a tool for measuring cost savings and controlling legal expenditures. Some companies have started to leverage the utilization ratio for other progressive initiatives, such as their company diversity and inclusion requirements. I have yet to see diversity and inclusion requirements included on cost estimates for clients, but I expect this aspect of utilization ratios will also, at some point, be included as part of a client's cost estimate request to a law firm.

## Challenging the traditional legal model

As mentioned earlier, the legal marketplace has undergone a lot of changes since the "Great Recession", forcing corporate executives to become increasingly cognizant of how they spend their shareholders' money. This is especially true for many legal departments, which are considered to be expensive cost centers. Fiscal prudence is top of mind for many general counsels and legal ops folks as they are looking to firms not just for expert legal advice and excellent service delivery, but also for cost-savings opportunities whenever and wherever possible.

Traditionally, the most senior timekeepers at a firm would enjoy the most complicated and highest revenue-generating corporate matters, with minimal time billed by less expensive professionals. This type of traditional revenue-generating model has been the status quo among many firms for decades now.

Economics is the major reason most firms do not delegate work to less expensive lawyers or administrative and clerical staff. Many administrative support staff do not directly bring in revenue for a law firm. Clients need to stay vigilant about how associates bill their time because many are now billing time for work previously performed by non-lawyers. If a firm is required to delegate greater quantities of work to more junior professionals, there may be a greater temptation, in the interest of law firm profitability, to increase the quantity of time required to perform a task or to bill clerical-type tasks that once were never passed on to the client. It is worth reiterating that clients need to closely scrutinize cost estimates utilizing less experienced professionals such as associates, in order to understand what those professionals will be responsible for and the quantity of time that they will be expected to bill.

For years now, there has been a debate about the value that junior associates bring to a matter in terms of work experience and quality. Clients seem to be pushing for more seasoned professionals, not junior associates fresh out of law school, to work on their matters. Many corporate clients have gone so far as to impose staffing requirements that restrict the utilization of first and second year associates on any of their matters because they do not see any substantive value coming from these two classes of associates. Consequently, some clients take the position, when reviewing staff utilization ratios in cost estimates, that they will not pay the cost of having to train junior associates on their matters. Therefore, clients don't like to see inexperienced junior associates included as part of a law firm's cost estimate proposal.

*Figure 3: Profitability pyramid models.*

Progressive firms willing to adopt more client-centric approaches and focused on building strategic and value-generating partnerships have started to change their traditional profitability pyramid model (see Figure 3) to reflect the demands of their clients by placing more of a weighting towards more junior and mid-level professionals, giving them greater involvement on larger, more significant (i.e. revenue-generating) matters.

These types of value-building strategies and cost-conscious approaches build intrinsic value at a firm by passing the torch to mid-level associates. Clients want to see evidence of progressive utilization ratios on the cost estimates that firms provide because the change to utilizing less expensive professionals provides a more cost-effective approach for the client and a more progressive, long-term profitability model for the firm.

## Monitoring staff utilization ratio in cost estimates

Perhaps the easiest method of monitoring the staffing utilization ratio on a matter is to require that a law firm provide a staffing summary (see Figure 4) either prior to the start of the matter and/or at the end of the matter when a firm submits its invoice.

**Invoice law firm staff utilization ratio summary**

| Class | Total $ Billed | % Ratio/Matter |
|---|---|---|
| Associates | 45,300 | 75% |
| Clerks/Paralegals | 12,225 | 20% |
| Other | 3,250 | 5% |
| Total | 60,775 | 100% |

*Figure 4: Invoice staff summary.*

Many corporate clients are utilizing their e-invoicing software to produce executive-type staffing summaries at the conclusion of their matters. The staffing summary aggregates all of the time billed by the individual timekeepers on an invoice and consolidates it into a snapshot, showing the total dollars billed along with a percentage ratio for each professional class of timekeepers.

The executive summary in Figure 5 helps illustrate how the workload on a matter was distributed amongst the professional classes and timekeepers at a firm. Such a summary can assist clients in making staff utilization determinations prior to or during the progress of a matter. Being able to see delegation information is important for clients that are cost-conscious and require firms to manage a matter within an assigned

**Executive summary**
**Law firm staff utilization ratio**

| Timekeeper | Ranking | Qty time | Rate | TTl billed |
|---|---|---|---|---|
| Angelo | Partner | 2 | 475 | 950 |
| Smithson | Partner | 1 | 445 | 445 |
| Lutz | Partner | 3 | 505 | 1,515 |
| Devon | Partner | 4 | 515 | 2,060 |
| Williamson | Partner | 5 | 480 | 2,400 |
| **Total associates** | | **15** | | **7,370** |
| | | | | |
| Frederick | Associate | 3 | 300 | 900 |
| Adamski | Associate | 11 | 375 | 4,125 |
| Bromovitz | Associate | 9 | 390 | 3,510 |
| Sheer | Associate | 9 | 400 | 3,600 |
| **Total Associates** | | **32** | | **12,135** |
| | | | | |
| | **Staffing ratio breakdown** | | | |
| **Partners** | | **15** | | **7,370** |
| **Associates** | | **32** | | **12,135** |

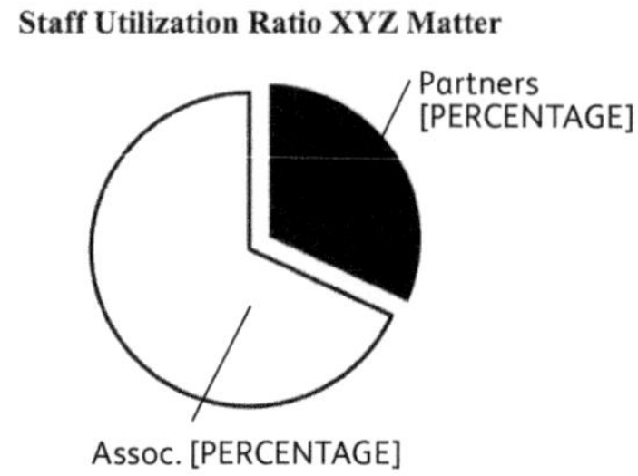


*Figure 5: Executive Summary.*

budget or when the firm is still billing its time based on an hourly rate. The staffing summary is a simple way to demonstrate whether a firm is meeting an assigned target set by the client or highlight simple transactional work that a firm can delegate to less expensive professionals, thereby saving the client money.

In some circumstances, a firm may not even be aware of the delegation issue or how out of sync its utilization ratio is from its client's need to control legal costs. Firms need to pay special attention to their utilization ratios and how they scale across their organization, leverage less expensive resources, and promote efficiencies for the greater good of their clients if they want to stay competitive and win more mandates.

For in-house legal departments that utilize panels of preferred law firms and have the ability to generate automated reports from their legal e-billing software, utilization reports offer meaningful insight into how effective a firm is in scaling its internal resources for the benefit of the client.

Clients should consider creating automated utilization ratio reports either monthly or yearly to analyze historical timekeeper billing data. This data may be invaluable in identifying trends or patterns of billing amongst specific professional classes. Staff utilization reports can also assist clients to conduct cross-firm comparisons with similar peer firms to determine which firms are the most proactive in delegating legal work to less expensive timekeepers or classes of legal professionals. Clients may even want to share their findings (anonymized, of course) with their panel firms to help drive change and incentivize them to utilize less expensive legal professionals.

## Measuring and monitoring work in progress (WIP) ratio

Another important factor to consider when implementing a cost estimate with a firm is a mechanism to measure and monitor the cost of work in progress as it relates to a law firm's cost estimate. I refer to this analysis as the work in progress ratio (WIP ratio).

The WIP ratio is a predetermined percentile, determined by the client, that acts as a threshold and that is typically correlated to the total value of a cost estimate or a specific fee cap. Once a firm reaches the WIP ratio, most clients will require that a firm contact the client to discuss what work is left to be completed before the firm can continue to do any additional work on the matter.

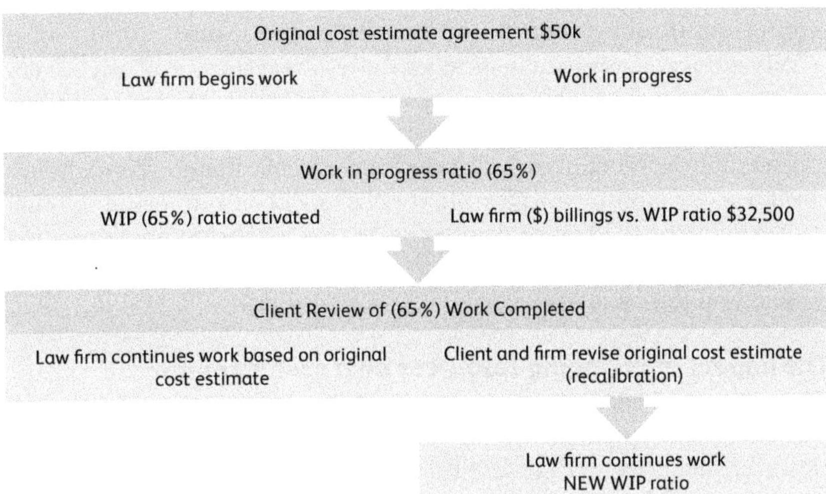


*Figure 6: WIP ratio.*

For example, Figure 6 illustrates that if a client determines that the total value of the cost estimate is to be $50,000 and the WIP ratio is 65 percent, then the client requires that the law firm will contact the client when the firm determines that it has completed 50 percent of the cost estimate or the equivalent of $32,500 in terms of work effort billed on the matter. Contravening the WIP ratio requirement, for any reason, may result in monetary or other types of penalties for the firm.

The WIP ratio acts like a self-imposed alert mechanism, or a checkpoint, to allow the client (at a predetermined juncture in the course of a matter) and the firm to pause and reassess the work effort on the matter up to a particular point in time. The WIP ratio allows both parties to understand where they are in terms of the overall cost estimate and if need be to reassess the scope of their engagement, recalibrate, and/or to revisit the original cost estimate as the client requires. This is especially important for clients who have engaged a new firm and are looking for a mechanism to assist the client with an opportunity to review and assess the work level of a firm part way through a cost estimate.

I have encountered many circumstances, especially on protracted complicated matters, where a law firm loses sight of a client's cost estimate and invariably exceeds it, only to have to face an uncomfortable discussion around overage after the firm has billed the client. Having a WIP ratio in place helps mitigate the occurrence of overages on legal matters and acts as a notification mechanism to review, question, or even challenge the work effort or expenses (to date) as they relate to matter scope, expectations, progress, and unforeseen variances.

WIP ratios are prevalent in most legal e-billing systems and can be very easily operationalized by minor configuration settings in an e-billing system. Clients simply need to ensure that they activate this type of functionality, especially on protracted and complicated matters where a client receives monthly invoices. In the absence of an automated solution to managing the WIP ratio, clients should always consider incorporating some level of staggered compliance monitoring to help manage their matters and the costs associated with those matters.

### The impact of changing resources on a cost estimate

Cost estimates, once approved, are typically static arrangements that, if agreed upon by all parties, form the basis of the pricing agreement. However, clients, as well as law firms, may want to revisit the cost estimate should the scope of the engagement change or become increasingly complex with unforeseen variables that require more time or additional resources.

Changing circumstances may create variances that ultimately affect the original cost estimate. Therefore, it is important for both parties to a cost estimate that they both understand the nature of the request and why an increase to the original proposed estimate is required. Clients will require details from a firm explaining the basis and rationale for any proposed changes. Conversely, law firms should ensure they understand how any proposed changes will impact the scope and any other components of a matter. Whenever possible, firms should be definitive in their change request proposals and avoid using ambiguous numbers and language such as "in the range of X%" or "in the range of X$ to X$" when proposing changes to the cost component of an estimate.

Over the years I have experienced multiple occasions of what I refer to as the "drive-by billing" phenomena, whereby professionals at a law firm look to fill up their monthly billing quota by contributing small quantities of time to multiple matters. Typically, drive-by billing brings little if any value to a matter at the client's expense.

Clients with e-billing software or access to AI tools should data mine their billing data so as to monitor how matters are staffed and whether they comply with staffing proposals that are included in any cost estimate strategy. Law firms should revisit their original cost estimates and ensure that they explain to their clients the cost implications of any change request on the staff utilization ratio in the cost estimate. Clients should be convinced that the need to include additional or new resources and the costs associated with the change request are necessary and add value to the matter.

## The benefits of using alternative fee arrangements in a cost estimate

Cost estimates are increasingly moving away from the hourly rate model and utilizing alternative fee arrangements (AFAs) and other value priced fee structures and strategies.

Clients are embracing a diversity of pricing options that allow them to manage and monitor their matters within a prescribed budget. For years many cost estimates were based simply on hourly rates, offering clients an understanding and an agreement as to the quantity of time (hours) various timekeepers would spend on a matter measured against the hourly rate they used to calculate the total price. Depending on the relationship with the client, the hourly rate may have been discounted from the law firm's commercial or street rate.

Anyone familiar with the legal marketplace knows by now that AFAs have been increasing in popularity with many clients for many years. Many clients today are looking for their cost estimates to include some type of AFA component. It's not uncommon for all types of AFAs to be included in a cost estimate. I have seen flat fee, block fee, risk/reward, blended rate, fee collars, and variations of task based billing arrangements included in various types of cost estimates. Perhaps the most popular and easiest AFAs that I have seen utilized in cost estimates have been the flat fee or fixed fee arrangement and tasked based billing arrangements.

Flat fee pricing offers the client an opportunity to negotiate a variety of work, all within the scope of one flat fee from the firm. Cost estimates that propose pricing for flat fees offer clients the following advantages:

- Simplest AFA pricing arrangements to manage for many business clients;
- Can be easily managed and maintained in a law firm's accounting software as well as a client's e-billing system to accommodate changes in scope as there is only one item (price) to change;
- Better than utilizing hourly rates as clients don't need to be concerned about staffing ratios (who does the work at a firm), how long and at what hourly rate, so long as the work product delivered meets the clients' standards;
- Certainty that the scope of engagement (all or part of it) will be covered off with one flat fee price; and
- Includes everything in the final cost estimate price. It's the ideal "all in" scenario for clients and firms.

If hourly rates need to be utilized in a cost estimate, many clients are turning to a negotiated blended hourly rate that allows the law firm to charge one "universal" rate for all of its services, regardless if it is a junior associate or a senior partner or clerk working on the client's matter.

Clients are attracted to the blended rate because it allows them to focus on one common rate, regardless of the professional working on the matter, as opposed to numerous timekeepers at different rates. Blended rates typically appear in cost estimates where a law firm wants to make things easier for a client to manage and where the rate is coupled to a flat fee arrangement. Law firms still want the flexibility to defer to an hourly rate should there be some sort of variances to address – something perhaps that the flat fee cost estimate did not account for and in circumstances where some extra work is needed but is outside of the flat fee arrangement.

Blended rates are calculated to represent the average hourly rate of all professionals either within a band, professional class (e.g. associates or partners), year of call or geographic area. Most times I have seen cost estimate blended rates separate the blended rate according to professional class (i.e. associates and partners) within a specific geographical area.

To give a client greater comfort around the blended rate, firms may want to suggest a cap on the number of hours (hours cap) that a firm will be allowed to bill against the blended rate. Anything that is anticipated above and beyond the established hours cap will require consent from the client in advance of the work being completed. This also provides the client with greater visibility into whether or not they need to provision extra funds in their budget should the firm be required to dip into the utilization of the blended hourly rate.

As mentioned before, the blended rate is commonly utilized for variances or assumptions that come out of left field for the firm. Allowing a firm the latitude to utilize the blended rate for any variances that need to be addressed allows for the matter to proceed uninterrupted without having the law firm delay work in order to obtain permission from the client. Matter continuity and progress are especially important when a client has set tight deadlines for its firm. Blended rates incorporated into cost estimates afford firms the flexibility to have their professionals work uninterrupted, so that clients get the benefit of one rate regardless of the professional class.

Task based billing arrangements are another AFA that clients have increasingly been attracted to and can easily be included in any cost estimate proposal. Clients looking to manage their costs by identifying individual tasks, milestones, and project objectives can all be segregated, defined, and negotiated to arrive on a flat fee for that specific task.

Law firms favor task based billing because it segregates a large matter into portions and firms can bill their time according to the successful outcome of a particular task as opposed to having to wait for the completion of an entire matter (e.g. contract negotiation or a litigation matter) that can sometimes become drawn out and/or protracted. In addition, task based cost estimates offer clients the visibility into a firm's success as the firm progresses through a matter and defines exactly the cost for the completion of that specific task, regardless of which professional is working on the matter.

Whether it's a flat fee, blended hourly rate, or task based billing proposal that is being leveraged in a cost estimate, both the client and law firm need to ensure that they mutually understand and agree upon how the specific pricing arrangement is to work. Both parties need to understand and reach a consensus also on what tasks or specific work are to be included in either a task or overall work effort as well as a mutual agreement on the description of the work effort (i.e. scope).

Like any other cost estimate, if AFAs are being used, there needs to be clear communication as to how variances and/or any assumptions are to be dealt with. In short, if AFAs are utilized as part of a cost estimate strategy, it's worth noting that their utilization, and success, is only one component of that strategy that is co-dependent on other factors already mentioned. AFAs simply offer up a different and perhaps easier approach to managing legal costs that a client would like defined as part of their cost management strategy.

## Third party vendor costs

There may be situations in the course of a matter that require a firm to utilize third party vendors (TPVs) such as co-counsel, experts, or other types of service providers. The costs associated with TPVs are typically billed to clients in the form of disbursements. Firms prefer to exclude TPV costs from any cost estimates as the need to engage a TPV, for whatever purpose, may not be entirely definitive and quantifiable prior to a matter commencing. Nevertheless, some clients may want greater comfort, for budgeting purposes, to scope TPV costs, and may require a firm to quantify TPV costs even if it is only as a rough estimate. In such circumstances both parties to the cost estimate should treat TPV costs as a variance expense to be utilized only after a client has provided the firm with their approval.

## How to treat disbursements in a cost estimate

Most cost estimates that I have reviewed have almost always excluded disbursements from the proposal. If there are to be any ancillary charges, administrative overhead, or even TPV costs, they are typically dealt with outside of a cost estimate. Lawyers proposing cost estimates are almost always laser focused on their work effort and not on any ancillary costs associated with a matter. I have encountered numerous scenarios where lawyers have quoted me an estimate and excluded disbursements, thinking that the disbursements would be nominal, but in fact turned out to be sizeable costs that impacted the overall cost estimate.

Ultimately, as part of any comprehensive cost estimate and to mitigate against any cost surprises, a law firm should provide the client with some sort of reasonable expectation around additional disbursement costs. If they are based on historical experience or if the costs are transactional in nature or are tied to civil procedures or some type of tariffs, disbursement costs should not be too difficult to calculate and provide to the client.

Moreover, data-savvy firms understand the type of disbursements that they typically charge on highly transactional or routine matters. In those types of engagements, clients have come to expect that the firm will include the cost of disbursements as a line item in the cost estimates that they propose to their clients.

Depending on the type of engagement or legal matter, there are many different types of disbursements and levels of cost. In the end, clients need to be cognizant of what to expect in regard to their cost estimate and how disbursements may ultimately impact the cost estimate of a particular matter. In some types of matters (e.g. litigation, insolvency, e-discovery, trademark etc.) disbursements may add up quickly and potentially derail a client's earlier cost estimate.

Clients who do not have a disbursement policy in place with their external counsel should be cognizant of how a law firm bills for its ancillary expenses. Most firms today have opted to simply charge a flat percentage rate against the total value of an invoice or cost of a matter to cover off extra expenses. While I am not particularly fond of this approach, I understand why a firm would take it as it is an easy method of managing ancillary expenses for a firm. Thrifty clients have come to challenge firms on this practice and even fewer accept the practice because many feel it is unfair and unjustified and does not reflect the actual disbursements incurred on a matter. As one client once told me, "Why should I be responsible for paying for the firm's leaseholds or expensive office décor? That has nothing to do with the actual disbursements charged on my matter."

## The importance of a communication strategy

At the heart of any cost estimate is a mutual agreement on the part of the client and law firm to honor the proposed cost estimate as the basis for a pricing agreement. Therefore, both parties need to fully understand and agree upon all of the components of the cost estimate and how those components are to be dealt with in the form of a communication strategy.

Establishing a clear communication strategy that outlines the circumstances in which both the law firm and client are expected to communicate is an integral part of any cost estimate, especially in circumstances where there is a protracted or complicated matter that has a high risk of variances occurring or frequent questions arising. Without a communication strategy, it is not uncommon to find circumstances in which both parties to an engagement may make false assumptions based on assumed expectations.

For example, a client may expect a law firm to call him or her to discuss a variance that has surfaced, but the law firm may assume that it has a green light to deal with variances without having to involve the client. This type of situation inevitably results in a disconnect, which can quickly become costly for a client and even for the firm if the client refuses to pay for unauthorized legal work that is tied to the variance.

Communication is the simplest element of a good cost estimate; it should not be overlooked, misinterpreted, or outright ignored. Having a communication strategy in place reduces the potential for delays in dealing with matter uncertainties and changes in scope, staffing, and simple contact points on a matter. Including a communication strategy in a cost estimate reduces the risk of ambiguity and assumptions and helps support cost estimates by adding greater certainty to how a matter is to be managed, including expectations around cost deliverables and ultimately whether or not value is delivered. Built into the communication plan should be how often a client expects scheduled status updates on a matter, or how quickly a firm should forward clarification questions to a client ahead of any additional (out of scope) work that is required. In short, a communication strategy helps manage expectations for both parties involved in the matter.

Clients with large legal departments should also outline which parties are to be contacted by listing a primary and secondary point of contact and the preferred method of contact (e.g. email, phone, or even text messaging). For large protracted matters, clients may want to establish regularly scheduled meetings or conference calls to have a firm communicate updates on cost estimates and/or budgets.

Recalibrating a cost estimate after a matter has commenced is not uncommon and should be incorporated into the communication strategy of every cost estimate. Both parties to the cost estimate should be invited to share their opinion or feedback on the progress to date, which may also include feedback on a law firm's performance, timeliness, staffing, or costs. Clients may find that they want to expand or reduce a matter in scope. All of this may inevitably have an impact on the agreed-upon cost estimate and may require a recalibration of the matter itself.

Communication strategies act as checkpoints to see how a matter is progressing and should be viewed as constructive practices in the scope of the engagement. Both the client and firm benefit from having set out mutually agreed-upon expectations around communication before beginning a matter.

## The criticality of properly defining and understanding scope

The importance of defining expectations and communicating what exactly it is that a law firm is engaged on before the start of a matter is critically important for all parties. In terms of identifying legal costs and defining budget expectations, understanding the scope of a matter clearly and without any ambiguity is crucial to the success of any cost estimate.

All cost estimates are typically based on the scope of the engagement and/or the terms that a client has set out for the engagement with a law firm. The scope is by far the most critical element of the cost estimate because it defines the business expectations between the client and the law firm and provides the basis on which any pricing arrangement is agreed upon. Therefore, it is vitally important for clients to define (in writing) the parameters and expectations around the engagement, removing as much ambiguity as possible in order to allow a law firm to provide as accurate a cost estimate as is possible.

I have unfortunately all too often seen scope instructions from clients to be less than optimal or plagued with ambiguities. The narrative that is used to describe the scope should be clear and definitive. On large protracted matters, the scope may include a multitude of tasks. Those tasks should be clearly defined to give the law firm as much information as is possible for the firm to make an informed and accurate assessment and reliable cost estimate. If the narrative that is used to describe the scope is not written well or contains ambiguity, the risk increases that a law firm may not present an accurate cost estimate to the client and that, at some point in time, both parties may be forced to unexpectedly revise the cost estimate, which creates issues for both sides.

A properly defined scope statement should include the following components:

- A clear statement of work, including the objective of the matter and a defined plan if the matter is complex;
- Detailed description of any significant milestones or tasks with a prescriptive narrative for each;
- A list of any known variances to be excluded from the matter;
- Deadline dates for either the entire matter or milestone tasks if required;
- A mutually agreed process for change requests and dealing with variances; and
- A detailed list and description of assumptions, their additional cost, and expectations of how they are to be acted on and included into the scope of the matter.

## The importance of communication during the cost estimate process

Defining the scope of engagement is critically important to the success of any cost estimate. Whether it's the definition of a specific task or milestone, or a narrative defining a multitude of expectations and deliverables, such as a project or book of business, defining the objective of a legal mandate in specificity or using simple language to describe the legal services that are required is fundamental to the success of any engagement relationship as it increases the odds (exponentially) of success for the cost estimate and ultimately the matter.

Unfortunately, this is not always the case. All too often I have seen extremely competent lawyers (both in-house and externally) as well as seasoned business clients drop the ball when it comes to communicating their cost estimate business requirements or the scope of a matter. When things go wrong or expectations (usually the client's) are not met, people inevitably look for an explanation to try to understand why there was a disconnect or why legal costs exceeded expectations. I believe the answer lies within a basic tenet in the client/lawyer relationship – communication.

In my experience I can attest that there is a lot of room for improvement for both the buyer (client or in-house counsel) and the seller (law firms) of legal services when it comes to communication. Unfortunately, the lack of discipline and accuracy around cost estimate communication and defining the scope of engagement accurately is not a new phenomenon. In fact, poor communication has been at the root of many challenges and adversely impacted client and law firm relationships for many decades.

Part of the reason for this rests with clients who habitually predicate their cost estimate on the assumption that the firms they hire will not have any difficulty understanding the client's instructions. Clients who have adopted this mindset typically do not second guess their communication strategy or question whether they have properly described a task in their cost estimate or whether their cost estimate includes all of the relevant information a firm will need to complete its work.

When lack of, or suboptimal, direction is coupled with a failure to communicate, regardless of which party is to blame, the integrity of the cost estimate is undermined and all parties inevitably suffer. In my experience, more often than not, it has been the client (and not the firm) that has to take responsibility for the deficiencies around communication in regard to cost estimates that fail to meet expectations.

Large corporate environments can be extremely busy, with multiple internal business partners, each with differing views and priorities, competing for assistance from finite and taxed in-house legal resources. Because of this, many internal business clients may be left on their own to engage firms without the screening benefit offered by in-house counsel. Consequently, at the risk of sounding condescending, many business clients just don't know how to write or describe engagement instructions or define scope or business requirements properly. Given this type of environment, it's no wonder that for many clients the only two components of a cost estimate that get any attention are the price tag and delivery date. Many other items and information that a firm may require or that may be of essential importance to a matter is either overlooked in the scope description and not communicated to the firm or left to the firm to make costly assumptions that result in unexpected overages.

Over the years I have encountered repeated situations where some clients just didn't understand the relevance of information and omitted certain documents in their cost estimate or engagement instructions. Firms, as well, have told me that they have encountered situations, which I consider to be shocking, where clients have selectively (and intentionally) chosen not to include certain facts or material as part of the scope because they thought the material to be irrelevant to the matter or that the client wanted to reduce the firm's workload and save money by reducing the cost estimate. I don't think any amount of temporary cost savings can justify putting a company's reputation at risk.

Furthermore, aside from intentional omissions, there may also be some circumstances where clients may unknowingly and unintentionally omit critical information (e.g. business purpose, strategy, requirements, legal and operational risk, expectations) that may be extremely pertinent to a matter and relevant to the work that a law firm is doing on a matter. Such omissions or deficiencies in proper communication will inevitably impact how a cost estimate is composed. This is why I have always recommended, especially for large corporate environments, that clients implement a centralized and managed approach to cost estimates, where internal legal ops professionals manage and oversee the outtake as well as the intake cost estimate process. Having a second set of eyes, by trained professionals, ensures that any cost proposals are composed properly, include the right information, and can be tracked for successful outcomes.

## Defining scope

When it comes to defining scope, clients should ask themselves whether or not they have defined the engagement in realistic terms and provided enough information to the law firm that allows the firm to act on that information in a definitive and comprehensive manner. Whenever possible, a firm should deliver the best legal advice within the cost parameters of the matter without having to make any costly assumptions.

I have experienced many cost estimate scenarios where clients neglected to include complete information or narratives around scope and provided law firms with extremely ambiguous language that consequently resulted in an overage and a lot of finger pointing. Clients need to be cognizant of how they structure and communicate their business requirements or scope of engagement to the firms they hire. They should look to define the scope of engagement clearly and, where possible, without any ambiguity. Becoming more prescriptive in their approach may ultimately benefit the client. I think too much information is always better than too little, as too much will most certainly reduce the risk for assumptions and potential overages on a cost estimate. Too little information, on the other hand, increases the risk for a firm to have to make assumptions and potentially do work that the client may view as unnecessary or outside of their authorized budget parameters. If such is the case, a firm may be asked to write down their work in order for the client to stay within a prescribed budget.

Whenever possible, clients should also look to leverage their legal ops folks when developing cost estimates. As mentioned earlier, legal ops professionals can add tremendous value to the cost estimate process. They can also assist business clients and in-house lawyers with developing business requirements, defining and quantifying tasks, and producing key deliverables and expectations.

Perhaps the most obvious resources clients can leverage for assistance with writing and developing their cost estimates is their in-house counsel team, who frequently work closely with internal business clients. In fact, because in-house counsel typically are familiar with internal business processes, they are increasingly finding themselves in a liaison role between the business client and the law firm. It's not uncommon for in-house lawyers to have to sacrifice their valuable time interceding to either clarify a business client's original instructions or altogether rewriting them. I have heard many firms lament about how internal businesspeople woefully lack the proper skill set to write operational requirements or instructions around scope and moreover how they are challenged when it comes to understanding operational risk in regard to the legal matters they have engaged the firm on. This business handicap or deficiency translates into poorly written instructions and creates operational risk for the client's organization. In-house legal counsel can help mitigate any business client deficiencies and complement them with clear and definitive language when defining scope in a cost estimate. In-house counsel understand the client's business requirements, terminology, risk appetite, and budget appetite – all of which, on significant or strategic matters, is critically important in defining expectations.

As for business clients, they should never assume to understand the legal implications of certain business decisions. Businesspeople are not lawyers. Lawyers are trained to understand the law and mitigate against risk. Therefore, leaning as much as possible on internal legal resources when writing and defining scope is definitely an advantage, provided the instructions are well written, clear, and definitive.

If there is a need to accommodate variances, this should be clearly communicated somewhere in the project scope or as an addendum in the cost estimate. Both the client and the law firm are responsible for ensuring that all communication on a matter is clear and each should challenge the other if it isn't.

Some time ago I was speaking at a conference on approved counsel management and was part of a panel discussing my thoughts on the business of law and how the delivery of legal services has changed in the past decade. As part of the Q&A session I was asked by a young lawyer what she could do to build and improve her client relationships. I responded by saying, "Many lawyers have been trained in the law but very few have invested a similar amount of time and energy in learning how to communicate, listen, and understand what their clients need. Every client is unique and may require different approaches and responses. Making assumptions and generalities risks alienating some clients who may think their business or needs are unique. So treat your clients like they are special, anything less than that may make them feel unappreciated and pedestrian (undervalued) in a transactional relationship."

This is especially true when it comes to defining scope and understanding the needs of the client at the time of engagement. For example, even though a firm may have worked on hundreds of identical intellectual property matters, all that a new client cares about is to be made to feel like *they* are the firm's only (special) client.

Clients today are very business savvy and know when they are being marginalized or simply dismissed as less important. Every matter, regardless of size or value, and every engagement or interaction with a client is an opportunity to grow the relationship. Taking the time to understand the scope of the engagement with a client and not making any false assumptions reinforces the value and importance of the client's relationship to a firm. How a client is made to feel is sometimes more important than the value or size of a matter.

If I had to develop a cost estimate formula for service delivery it would look something like this:

**Hk + Pr + Ap / ExCom + No Surprises = Special**

Any cost estimate that develops as part of the relationship should reflect the firm's historical knowledge (Hk), pragmatic recommendations/ proposal (Pr) at an affordable price (Ap). All of this underpinned with an excellent communication (Excom) strategy and an assurance that there will not be any (cost) surprises.

"Hk + Pr + Ap / ExCom + No Surprises = Special" is by no means a magical formula, yet many firms continue to struggle to deliver all or some components of this formula in the cost estimates that they deliver.

### The law firm's responsibility in defining scope

I have discussed to some extent how the client's inability to communicate and define scope effectively is a significant contributing factor to why cost estimates fail. But it is not always the fault of the client. As the other principal party to a cost estimate agreement, firms share equal responsibility for ensuring that communication is flowing properly during a cost estimate proposal or negotiation. Therefore, if things go wrong, firms too should share an equal amount of fault.

In any cost estimate discussion and/or negotiation it is the firm, just like the client, that must agree to the cost estimate proposal as the basis of the engagement arrangement. Whether a client understands it or not, the law firm has an obligation to challenge a cost estimate if it is unfair, risky, or simply just not realistic and has a high probability of failing or having to be revised later in time. This is especially true when it comes to highly transactional matters where a firm may have years of experience in managing similar matters and knows intrinsically how much a matter should cost and whether or not any variances may come into play.

A good firm will share all of their insight and experience with their client when proposing a cost estimate. After all, ideally it's in their best interest. Firms that are reluctant to speak up or to challenge a client's cost estimate position may ultimately be risking their relationship and/or any future mandates if the client is at some point dissatisfied and looks to hold the law firm responsible for not speaking up or challenging the original cost estimate sooner.

I also think that part of the problem, as it relates to communication, has to do with some firms assuming that the client has gotten it right and that what the client has described (in terms of scope) must be completely accurate as the firm assumes that the scope description is based on the client's real life, day-to-day understanding and expertise in managing their own business, operational issues or even specific business requirements. Many firms make a false assumption that the client is right or knows their business requirement best, when that may not necessarily be true. There may be issues or gaps in understanding legal issues correctly and consequently the client's approach to a cost estimate may be flawed and doomed to fail right from the outset. Other times, the business folks (i.e. the client) running the business may not be the best suited to define what it is they need from the firm. In such circumstances, firms need to step up, speak up, and voice their concerns or questions to help the client better understand the potential for risk or additional costs if the matter or scope is not defined properly.

Firms may be engaged to provide advice on a particular issue, but they should also make the client aware of any peripheral issues that may impact the scope. Sometimes it should be the firm that instructs the client on what the real legal issue is, or where the risk lies in the client's business model. In other words, firms must be prepared to challenge their clients or question the business logic around any legal issue. The communication and exchange will be well worth it in defining the scope of the engagement and how the cost estimate fits into that engagement.

Surprisingly, this may not always be true. I believe that many firms don't question their clients and assume that what the client has provided in terms of instructions or a description on a cost estimate template is accurate. Herein lies the first issue as many external counsel have in fact had mixed experiences, at the very least inconsistent, with how poorly clients define scope or business requirements.

Some lawyers have expressed to me that business clients are the worst when it comes to defining business requirements. Typically in large corporations, the procurement group will be tasked with engaging external counsel and managing mandates and the engagement process. Herein lies the second issue as procurement acts as the intermediary between the line of business and the law firm. Procurement is tasked with writing up the scope details and negotiating the engagement, and whether they involve the line of business "experts" or not, firms act on the instructions they receive from the liaison. Procurement folks are experts at what they do and should not be faulted or blamed for any missteps as legal services are different from any other service providers that they typically deal with, including external consultants and accounting vendors. My experience has taught me that, unfortunately, many company procurement groups are not necessarily the best suited experts within a corporate environment to manage law firm relationships, including working on cost estimates, as they don't have the same level of experience and skills that would be found in subject matter experts like legal ops experts typically residing in the legal department. Unfortunately, there are still many large companies that continue to delegate the responsibility and oversight, including development of cost estimates, to procurement departments where invariably clients receive mediocre results and struggle with cost containment issues.

Progressive companies with advanced legal departments recognize their limitations and deficiencies around scope writing and insist that legal ops professionals be the ones to close this gap. Still other companies continue to rely on their law firms to assist business folks with writing and defining business requirements that ultimately become the basis of a cost estimate proposal. It's a bit unorthodox and has a twist of irony, but if it works and ensures everyone understands the scope properly, so be it.

I believe that, when hired by a client, every lawyer – especially seasoned lawyers who have had a lot of historical experience – should probe and even go so far as to challenge the client on the completeness and accuracy of how they defined their scope. There is nothing wrong with questioning a client's understanding of scope and assisting them with determining whether or not there are to be any assumptions or variances priced into a cost estimate. Cost conscious clients in today's market welcome such value added servicing, and many have come to expect it from the firms that they hire.

In today's legal marketplace, firms should pay extra attention to their communication strategy. If they don't have one, they should develop one and ensure that it is part of how they deliver their legal services to their clients. Having a discussion and mutual understanding on the details of a cost estimate and/or the overall engagement prior to the work commencing is constructive as well as proactive and mitigates the risk of any disconnect or cost surprises.

Both in-house counsel and external counsel, as well as business clients, are responsible for ensuring that all parties to the cost estimate understand each other's role and responsibilities, the scope of the engagement, timelines, and the pricing arrangement. There should not be any ambiguity. Unfortunately, this is not always the case and in many instances is easier said than done.

## The unpredictability of "scope creep" and accounting for variances

Perhaps the most frustrating challenge of any cost estimate exercise is having to account for the unpredictability of variances that may cause the scope of a matter to shift or change. There can be a variety of reasons for this occurring depending on the variables or composition of a matter. Many times, changes in scope cannot be managed because of extraordinary factors that are beyond a client's control.

Commercial contract law highlights a practice area that can be fraught with variances and even the best thought-out cost estimates can go sideways due to unexpected variances. In reviewing and assessing large corporate vendor agreements, clients will usually involve their in-house counsel teams to work in collaboration with their procurement teams to rewrite and restructure master service agreements. These types of matters inevitably require a large degree of negotiation with the external supplier that consequently requires many unexpected and unforeseen contract edits.

Large class action litigation is another example of a practice area that can be highly complex, unpredictable, and very costly because of unpredictable and numerous motions and e-discovery costs. Unexpected litigation variances or assumptions that have not been planned for can have disastrous consequences on clients' internal budget expectations. I have heard repeatedly from both law firms and in-house counsel that it is next to impossible to define cost estimates for class action matters. This is unfortunately not true.

I have managed to work on numerous successful cost estimates for clients involving large class action matters. Developing successful cost estimates with regards to large class actions begins by partnering with the right law firm and experts in litigation who understand how to:

- Leverage technology and artificial intelligence tools;
- Data mine previous historical litigation information to uncover expected patterns in litigation;
- Leverage their own historical data;
- Staff resources efficiently; and
- Lastly, define reasonable assumptions and price those assumptions (clearly) for clients to see in their cost estimate using key phases and tasks.

In today's marketplace it is no longer acceptable for in-house counsel to say to their internal clients that they cannot develop a reasonable cost estimate simply because of the complexity of a matter.

Regardless of the matter, practice group, or complexity of a matter, planning and defining scope are critical to managing expectations and preparing for the unexpected. If it is anticipated that the cost estimate will be significantly impacted by variances, then clients should work with their law firm to develop a game plan to account for those assumptions. Developing and incorporating some type of scope addendum or scope statement that addresses the costs associated with such scenarios may at the very least alert both the client and law firm to how changes in scope are to be handled.

Clients and law firms may not be able to identify and account for every variance on a matter, but experienced firms can certainly add value to a matter by alerting their client to the possibility of certain events or processes the firm expects to take place based on the firm's educated assumptions and historical experience. Clients are increasingly looking for firms that can bring that type of historical experience (backed up by historical data of course) to their relationship as opposed to allowing a client's matter to unfold. The latter scenario would not bode well for both the client and the law firm. Scope addendums may also help a client in understanding (and preparing) how the cost estimate may potentially have to absorb the utilization of additional law firm resources, additional legal work, changes to the staffing model, additional costs, changes in timelines and even a recalibration of the original legal strategy should the variables be significant.

## Dealing with cost estimate overages

Nothing tarnishes a relationship more than a lack of trust or suspicion that something is not right. When a cost estimate has been agreed upon, there should not be any surprises in terms of overages or ancillary costs that were never scoped, discussed, or included in the original cost estimate. Over staffing, unnecessary and unauthorized legal work, or working off assumptions are examples that inevitably result in unwelcome cost overages that erode trust between clients and law firms.

Whether it's because of poor communication, missing information, or unforeseen variables, firms may from time to time exceed a mutually agreed upon cost estimate. In my experience most overages that I have encountered have been attributable to either poor (client) communication or false (law firm) assumptions.

If a firm has exceeded a cost estimate (without the client's knowledge and permission) and the overage is significant, the firm should be prepared to explain why they exceeded the original cost estimate. How a client reacts to the overage depends on the client, the depth of their relationship, and of course the explanation from the firm around the overage.

I would expect that a reasonable explanation on the part of a firm will be met with a similar response from the client. This is especially true if the extra work effort was ultimately of value and benefit to the client and their organization. The client in the end has to decide if the overage is worth paying for. If a firm cannot get the client to accept and understand the value of the extra work, then the firm should be prepared to write off or reduce the overage amount. What clients don't want to see is a firm disregarding their original instructions and making false (costly) assumptions that force the client to have to negotiate the value of the unnecessary legal work.

Sometimes clients will misinterpret the scope of an engagement and under appreciate the legal risk involved. Business clients are not typically lawyers so it is understandable how this can happen. Clients in these circumstances should look favorably on their firms and weigh the value of the added work versus cost. If in the end there is true value, there should be no question of assuming the overage for the greater good of the client's company and the relationship with the firm. Firms should not be penalized and asked to write down receivables for legitimate and value driven work. Both the client and the law firm should always try to reach an amenable and fair conclusion in regard to any overage on a cost estimate.

Some clients may accept the fact that the extra legal work and costs were absolutely necessary but, because of budget constraints, they cannot approve the overage. In such circumstances a firm should consider some sort of adjustment or partial write down and perhaps look to meet the client halfway on covering the overage costs. This cushions the blow somewhat for the client, allows the firm to still be compensated (albeit partially), and most importantly demonstrates a commitment and sensitivity to any existing or future relationship the firm may have with the client.

Regardless of the circumstances surrounding a cost estimate overage, if a firm failed to contact a client prior to doing additional work and/or failed to follow a mutually agreed upon cost estimate or other terms of engagement, a firm should not be surprised to be challenged by a client on the overage. If it's a surprise, clients will automatically ask a firm to explain and justify why the firm exceeded the original cost estimate.

I have seen numerous times where firms have had to write down significant legal fees because the firm thought that the non-lawyer (i.e. business client) didn't understand the importance/risk/scope/legality of the issue and disregarded a client's instructions, or simply just made false assumptions without first checking with the client. It can be very costly for a firm if a client doesn't see the added value of the extra legal work that resulted in the overage or if the client feels that the firm contravened their terms of engagement. After all, one of the primary objectives of a cost estimate is to avoid surprises, especially around pricing and final legal costs.

Regardless of the reason for the overage, I believe that, in almost every scenario, a firm can stay within a mutually agreed upon cost estimate and avoid an overage if the following best practices are followed:

- Communicate any questions and concerns regarding a mandate to the client early in the engagement process;
- If variances surface in the course of a matter, ensure those variances have been accounted for in the original cost estimate; if not, regroup and revisit the cost estimate with the client;
- Understand upfront the "what if" scenarios, and ensure the client understands what legal work needs to be done and at what cost;
- Follow any mutually agreed upon budget requirements such as notifying the client at a specific dollar threshold (e.g. WIP ratio is activated);
- Ensure that you keep within the agreed staffing model and manage professionals accordingly (remember, clients hate surprises);
- Manage third party expenses and disbursements, alerting the client to any unexpected costs prior to incurring them;
- Do not make unilateral assumptions; contact and discuss any concerns directly with the client ahead of any extra work that you think needs to be done;
- Propose options for the client and revisit and recalibrate cost estimates if necessary;
- Whenever possible, leverage and recycle previous (historical) work product (and let the client know that you did this – they love to see how you saved them money); and
- Work efficiently and effectively for your client (this is in your best interest – it's not just about churning out the hours. If the client sees you are efficient, the work will flow to you).

### The blame game – dealing with law firm "fault bias"

Clients are focused on hiring the most experienced experts at the right price. Once all of the components of the cost estimate have been mutually agreed upon, there is an expectation (based on mutual trust and good faith) that both parties will honor the cost estimate. Unfortunately, equitable responsibility is not always at the forefront of many clients' minds when their cost estimates begin to falter.

I think there is long held suspicion in the legal community that there is what I refer to as a "fault bias" amongst corporate clients who are quick to fault a law firm whenever cost estimate setbacks occur, because in some clients' minds the onus of responsibility always rests with the firm to prove otherwise.

I think that the fault bias with some clients may be a consequence of a larger (post-Great Recession) paradigm shift that has taken place in the legal marketplace. Law firms no longer have absolute control over the legal market supply. That shift in control has moved to clients who now control the demand and especially how and what work is sourced. With the control of how the legal work is sourced, and to which firm, squarely in the hands of many clients, they have introduced high expectations and requirements around service delivery.

Providing excellent customer service, timeliness, quality, communication, and reasonable and predictable pricing are some of the basic characteristics other industries have used for many years to measure, monitor and manage their service providers. The legal marketplace has started to catch up to these practices and has consequently undergone a paradigm shift whereby it has finally realized that lawyers are in the business of law, which includes the importance of meeting the clients' high expectations and service requirements.

So it's not surprising that when billings exceed original cost estimate expectations, the fault bias is triggered and clients naturally look to their law firms to explain the overage. If the overage is a surprise to the client, then it is far from being a *fait accompli* in today's marketplace as many clients have zero tolerance for surprises, especially those that can have an adverse impact on a client's established budget.

If a firm has exceeded a cost estimate (without the client's knowledge and permission) and the overage is significant, the firm should be prepared to explain why they exceeded the original cost estimate. How a client reacts to the overage depends on the client, the depth of their relationship, and of course the explanation from the firm around the overage.

I would expect that a reasonable explanation on the part of a firm will be met with a similar response from the client. This is especially true if the extra work effort was ultimately of value and benefit to the client and their organization. The client in the end has to decide if the overage is worth paying for. If a firm cannot get the client to accept and understand the value of the extra work, then the firm should be prepared to write off or reduce the overage amount. What clients don't want to see is a firm disregarding their original instructions and making false (costly) assumptions that force the client to have to negotiate the value of the unnecessary legal work.

Sometimes clients will misinterpret the scope of an engagement and under appreciate the legal risk involved. Business clients are not typically lawyers so it is understandable how this can happen. Clients in these circumstances should not be quick to fault a firm but instead look favorably on them and weigh the value of the added work versus cost. If in the end there is true value, there should be a question of assuming the overage for the greater good of the clients company and the relationship with the firm.

## How law firms should communicate overages to clients

Almost always, clients will look to the law firm to explain (and challenge) the circumstances around the overage (e.g. why the overage took place, contributing factors, scope creep, unexpected variances etc.).

When cost estimates are adversely impacted or when they go wrong, firms need to be prepared in advance of any discussions that may be uncomfortable for the client as well as the firm.

The following are some suggestions a firm may want to consider and incorporate into their communication strategy when approaching clients to discuss unplanned cost estimate overages:

1. **Apologize** – depending on the circumstances surrounding the overage and the firm's relationship with the client, some type of contrition may be required.

2. **Explain how and why the overage occurred** – this discussion needs to start with a verbal appreciation of the client's budgetary constraints, avoiding the blame game (even if it's the client's fault).

3. **Why the firm didn't advise the client in advance** – additional work and resources that result in supplementary costs may be necessary and explainable, but the client may only be focused on the failure to communicate these things ("why didn't you pick up the phone to advise me?"). The challenge will be to work through and demonstrate the additional value of the work and how it is justified (see points 7 and 8).

4. **Why the surprise** – why the extra work (variance) wasn't accounted for in the preliminary cost estimate or the firm's assumptions.

5. **Consider explaining the overage in the context of risk mitigation** – most clients will understand the overage if they realize the work was necessary to mitigate extra risk that may not have been included in the original scope and cost estimate.

6. **Don't assume the client will pay the overage** – regardless of the work effort.

7. **Be prepared to negotiate the cost of the extra work** – if it wasn't authorized, yet valuable to the client, consider (in the best interest of the relationship) reducing the overall cost of the work so as to cushion the impact to the client's budget.
8. **Consider writing off the overage and eating the cost** – easier said than done for some firms, but the client will be happy as they get the benefit of the extra work at zero cost and hopefully the client remembers the firm's sacrifice, loyalty, and determination to make things right in order to build the relationship.
9. **Hold your ground and make the client pay** – some clients are notoriously difficult and even incompetent when defining scope. Picking up the tab for a client's inability to properly define scope is fine if it happens once, but repeated occurrences should not be tolerated and bad clients should be held accountable and made to pay.

Regardless of how a firm approaches their client, the content of the message is critically important to the viability of the relationship with the client. Many times the overage can be logically explained and may in fact be required to mitigate risk for the benefit of the client. If done properly, most reasonable clients will accept and understand the benefit of a law firm's extra work effort and view the overage as a necessity.

Sophisticated buyers of legal services understand that fault and blame are secondary, or even further down the list, and not as important as understanding how to minimize a cost estimate overage and deal with it and learn to mitigate the issues that caused the overage so as to stop it from repeating itself in the future.

As already mentioned, clients do not look favorably on unexpected cost estimate overages, especially those where a firm chose to ignore instructions or made false assumptions. In such circumstances firms should be prepared to make some type of accommodation that results in writing down all or part of the work.

If the extra legal work that resulted in the overage is warranted and of significant value to the client, then whether or not it was authorized by the client, serious consideration should be given by the client to cover part or the entire overage. I think many clients who have established relationships with their firms, especially panel firms, recognize that their firms are looking out for their best interests and are not simply motivated to increase profit margins at any cost.

## Dealing with multiple clients and instruction points on a cost estimate

As part of any cost estimate process, the client should consider delegating a specific businessperson, legal ops specialist or business group to manage the compliance and oversight of the pricing arrangement. Should there be issues with the firm meeting the cost estimate or if the scope of the engagement changes, the firm will have only one business contact point to deal with when making the necessary revisions or updates to a cost estimate.

Managing the cost estimate through one gatekeeper reduces the risk that changes are made to the cost estimate without the knowledge of the legal department or other parties involved on the original cost estimate negotiation. This is especially important for firms that deal with large institutional clients and companies where legal operations are decentralized and there may be many differing (logistical) contact points. It is not uncommon for the legal department to negotiate or agree to a cost estimate and then later on a business partner somewhere else in the organization, without the legal department's permission or involvement, alters the scope of the engagement and, consequently, the value of the cost estimate.

# Chapter 3:
# Operationalizing a cost estimate strategy

Implementing a successful cost estimate strategy requires that the client first do their due diligence in understanding their existing cost management processes before creating the basic framework for their strategy. Understanding where a client is in terms of existing cost management processes and practices (e.g. LPM, AFAs, in-sourcing, tiering, staffing etc.) and what other tools they would like to deploy, such as cost estimates, to help them achieve their goals is important in laying the framework for creating a successful strategy. Many corporate clients are at different levels of evolution on the path to managing legal costs, law firms, and cost management strategies.

The framework should include an assortment of internal and external measurable management factors as part of the cost estimate strategy. The factors will help guide the client and the law firm in managing specific areas of the cost estimate strategy to ensure that it is implemented successfully. A few of those factors are listed below, along with some constructive questions for clients to consider when developing their framework.

## Internal factors

- Practice area – identify the practice areas that you routinely engage external counsel on and focus on those practice areas to implement a cost estimate strategy. If your company has multiple practice areas where you engage multiple firms, consider staggering the implementation of your strategy to one practice area at a time, involving only those firms that typically service those areas. Alternatively, you may also want to consider staggering the roll out to specific business or functional groups in your company that routinely engage external counsel.
- Complexity – review your list of practice areas and determine the complexity level (high or low) for each. For example, marketing matters or collection recovery work are typically routine,

consequently they may be designated as low complexity, versus tax litigation or regulatory matters, which may be considered highly complex. The complexity of the legal work that a firm is engaged on will determine the cost estimate requirements and the level of information a firm returns in its cost estimate proposal.

- Extraordinary matters – if you ever need to engage a firm on an extraordinary (i.e. black swan) legal matter (e.g. highly complex, perhaps class action or multiple entity legal issue) then consider creating a separate cost estimate template specific for that type of complex matter scenario. It's expected that a cost estimate template in such a scenario may contain more information for a law firm to return as part of its cost estimate proposal (see cost estimate templates below).
- Utilization – if you repeatedly utilize the same firms in a particular practice area then consider utilizing a simple transactional cost estimate template only once for each firm to cover off multiple engagements for the same type of matter (or practice area) as opposed to having multiple estimates with the same firm. If you are utilizing firms on an ad hoc basis and the matters are different in scope then a transactional cost template may be utilized. In both scenarios, clients should consider keeping the cost estimate process straightforward and uncomplicated to make the decision process as efficient as possible for both the firm and the client.
- Cost – having a basic understanding of costs with regards to a specific practice area creates a historical reference point for the client. The cost average can be either an hourly rate or flat or fixed fee for a matter or even a flat fee for a specific task on a matter. The objective of having an average allows the client to benchmark their cost average against the firm's proposal. It also allows the client to help establish the level of complexity to be assigned to a matter and the type of template to be utilized.
- Law firm status (panel or designated counsel status) – depending on the depth of your relationship (i.e. ad hoc versus a panel firm) and familiarity with the firm, the depth of the relationship may help guide you as to the type of cost template you may want to utilize. Having familiarity with a firm, and depending on the complexity of a matter, you may want to consider utilizing a less complicated cost estimate approach given the firm's familiarity with your processes and service delivery expectations, as opposed to a firm being

used for the first time, where you might want to consider a more prescriptive approach and detailed complex template.

- Resources – having a dedicated legal ops person to assist with the implementation of a cost estimate strategy and to manage the steady state and follow up with firms and internal business clients will help to ensure that the initiative is implemented successfully.
- Communication plan – ensure that all stakeholders to be impacted by the cost estimate strategy are notified ahead of the implementation of the strategy. This includes all panel firms if the strategy is to include all firms. Ensure that the communication plan includes instructions on how the cost estimate templates are to be utilized and describe the decision process.
- Executive buy – ensure that the project has executive and/or GC support and acceptance for the initiative, which will help with user compliance and utilization of cost estimates.
- Cost estimate template – depending on the complexity of a client's matters, a client may want to have least two cost estimate templates to utilize. One template should be for transactional type matters and would be very straightforward. The other template would be utilized for more complex matters and require more information from the firm.

## Case study – US insurance company

Some time ago I assisted a large US insurance company on implementing a company-wide cost estimate strategy. Prior to my assistance, the company had struggled to control costs and tried unsuccessfully to implement various cost containment and control measures with regards to its legal spend and how the company managed external law firms. Many of the issues that the company faced were attributable to a lack of executive buy-in and acceptance when it came to external counsel management, specifically many of the administrative components of a successful external management program. Things like implementing standard guidelines and a billing policy for all of their law firms, centralized and dedicated oversight of all law firms by a dedicated and trained legal ops professional, compliance monitoring, financial reporting and a central liaison for all law firms didn't really exist.

Historically, the company's procurement department was responsible for managing external counsel and therefore many of the processes and oversight reflected very generic vendor management practices that didn't apply to law firms or the legal industry. After a series of disastrous projects and escalating legal costs, the GC along with the company's executive leadership shifted all responsibility for external legal services from their procurement group to the GC's legal department. There was a lot of work to be done and we were very successful in implementing a number of cost savings initiatives.

One of those projects involved implementing a ubiquitous cost estimate strategy across the entire company for anyone who engaged an external law firm. The strategy also included centralizing all oversight compliance monitoring, tracking and reporting on the utilization of all cost estimate proposals. All of this came to be managed by a central legal ops professional and not a procurement person, junior clerk, or in-house counsel who was either inexperienced or didn't have the time to dedicate to the proper oversight of external counsel matters.

Central to the success of the initiative was executive buy-in and changing the company's mindset that cost estimates were a fundamentally important cost control tool and that every person at the company that engaged external counsel had a responsibility to ensure that they were spending the company's money wisely and thriftly on external counsel. Training and educating folks on how to utilize the cost estimate templates was pretty straightforward and uncomplicated. Added assistance and support from a legal ops professional was invaluable and knowing that there was a central liaison assigned and dedicated to external counsel matters was a significant bonus. All communication to the firm was centralized through the legal ops resource.

The cost estimate strategy helped give the client:

- A greater assurance and commitment from their firms that they would comply with a definitive pricing arrangement on any matter;
- A definitive framework detailing a plan for the delivery of legal services;
- A mutual confirmation and understanding of scope, instructions, and deliverables;
- transparency and insight into how a firm priced their proposals; and
- An opportunity to communicate how the client saw value being delivered in the work product that they paid for.

I didn't just want to create some type of administrative and perfunctory process. The intention was to create something that added value to the company and a mechanism and tool that in-house counsel, as well as their business partners, could utilize to control and manage their legal costs better.

In any work that I do for clients in regard to managing external legal service providers, I always try to give consideration to how any process change or new initiatives will impact the legal service providers. This was especially true on this project where I ensured that the importance of our project objectives and beliefs were communicated to the firms and the company's legal service providers. After all, they are an integral part of any service equation. I wanted to ensure that the panel firms also saw the added benefits not just to the company but also to the overall relationship the firms had with the client.

In our communications to the law firms I emphasized the importance of ensuring that the cost estimates that they returned to the client were backed up with real historical data and that, going forward, they should be prepared to be challenged by the client on the proposals that they submit. Also, I emphasized the need for every firm to look introspectively and try to do their best to operationalize the client's cost estimate template into their existing law firm processes so as to make their delivery response capabilities and timing for the client as efficient as possible.

The following list provides some of the benefits I highlighted to the client's law firms in order to help them understand the value of cost estimates to the overall relationship with the client. I emphasized how cost estimates can help:

- Foster reliability and dependability;
- Create a definitive framework for the client, and mitigate the risk of poor communication;
- Provide in-house lawyers and business partners with an increased sense of assurance, commitment, and predictability;
- Improve communication, define and agree on mutual expectations and deliverables;
- Helped build trust and client loyalty (priceless today in a homogenized marketplace);
- Reduce the frequency of cost overages occurring thereby reducing unnecessary fee write downs for the firm;

- Potentially increase the utilization of the law firm on other matters or in other practice areas; and
- Define and agree on a mutual understanding of how a client defines value.

The process took a bit of time to implement but is now an integral part of the company's processes and has resulted in a number of cost savings and control benefits as well as reducing the frequency of budget overages and law firms having to write down legal costs.

In the case study insurance company chart (Figure 7) I have highlighted some of the principal changes (Before and After) that took place at this company. Some of the items in the before section may resonate with some clients and hopefully can help to provide guidance for those looking to improve their processes around the implementation of a cost estimate strategy.

| Case study – insurance company | |
|---|---|
| **Background** | |
| **Before** | **After** |
| Company has a central General Counsel (GC) with a legal department of approximately 150 in-house lawyers, 30 clerks, and 20 admin. Utilizes a panel of approx. 300 law firms. There are many different internal business partners in the company who also have discretion to engage external firms on an ad hoc basis. | Senior executive and GC support for company-wide cost estimate strategy, managed by legal ops team reporting in to deputy GC. |
| **Before** | **After** |
| Cost estimates were utilized on an ad hoc basis by lawyers and business partners. | Specific cost estimate strategy implemented for any/all matters in excess of $25k, excluding transactional matters. |
| The utilization of cost estimates were not part of lawyers' regular modus operandi. | Mandatory cost estimates, compliance monitored by legal ops team and oversight of business partners' compliance. |
| Cost estimates considered an administrative chore and unnecessary business requirement with little value. | Value proposition and strategy designed and shared by GC. Changed company-wide mindset and dismissive behavior towards accepting and recognizing a process that holds value and is worth doing right. |

| Before | After |
| --- | --- |
| Cost estimates were not centralized in the company, no standard process or oversight or tracking. | Centrally managed, compliance tracked by legal department legal ops team. |
| Lawyers and business partners not really comfortable with asking for budgets or cost estimates. | Mandatory training and education roll out (lunch and learn sessions) for in-house counsel and self help TIPs guide for business partners rolled out re. the importance of cost estimates and their value to a matter in controlling costs. |
| Business partners only used ball park quotes for project budgets, which were rarely enforced.<br><br>"Budget quotes" were ambiguous, lacking substance and details. Mostly it was little more than a single sentence in the body of an email that provided a rough idea of what the cost would be on a matter. | Standardized (easy to use and understand) cost estimate template designed for all matters to be used by all firms - provides greater information (e.g. scope definition, task definition, timeline and highlights key deliverables, hourly rates, list of professionals staffing matter, total cost for matter, outlines assumptions with description and additonal costs and communication plan. |
| Assumptions, if described, were ambiguous in nature, identified multiple scenarios and did not describe when they would be used and if there was an extra cost. | Assumptions and variances require detailed description and plan as to how they will be added to a matter. In-house counsel must approve all assumptions in advance of any legal work being commenced on a matter. legal ops may be involved as required. |
| Law firms would sometimes use language like "supplementary costs" or "extra costs" around extra work but never describe in detail the extra work or how the work would be staffed. We rarely challenged our firms on these points.<br><br>Sometimes we would see premium pricing or a supplementary % rate assigned to a cost estimate where a firm expected to work on an assumption. | Any ambiguous or unexplained costs in a cost estimate proposal are not permitted and will be declined by either in-house counsel or business partners. |
| On larger matters we would receive cost estimates that were provided in the form of dollar ranges, with large deltas. The law firm invoices were always close to the top or above the dollar range in the deltas provided. | Dollar ranges are no longer permitted as they are too ambiguous. All cost estimate proposals must be definitive. If variances may be expected, these costs should be segregated as separate line items in the cost estimate. |

| Before | After |
|---|---|
| All of the quotes provided were always perfectly rounded numbers (e.g. 10k, 25k, 50k) that rarely provided any breakdown.<br><br>Our lawyers and our business partners would almost always accept the quote without any questioning or challenging our law firm. | Cost estimate information must be defined specifically to a task or milestone and the total expected cost for those items must be indicated. Firm is not permitted to "round up" their cost estimate or include a "price cushion" to account for variances or any assumptions. |
| If an overage occurred, most times our lawyers would accept it as a necessary consequence of the matter or scope and again rarely question or challenge a firm. | In-house counsel and our business partners are responsible for the legal costs on a matter. We have tried to instil the principle of "treat it as if it were your own personal money". This increased accountability has resulted in greater awareness and empowerment to ask questions. |

*Figure 7: Case study – before and after.*

## Law firm considerations

Just as important as internal client factors are factors that impact the law firm. Clients need to ensure that proper law firm factors and processes are considered to ensure the success of their cost estimate strategy. Some of these factors include:

- A detailed communication plan is in place, explaining to law firm staff the client's requirements in regard to the cost estimate;
- Scope – the scope of the engagement has been properly defined and mutually agreed upon by both the firm and the client;
- Dedicated resources – law firms should ensure that the right internal resources are utilized when developing a client's cost estimate. This goes well beyond just the lawyers who may be closest to the client. Legal ops folks as well as other experts (e.g. finance, project management, accounting, data analytics) should be included in developing the cost estimate;
- Reliable data – ensuring that the firm has done its due diligence with regards to its data analysis is critical to the cost estimate;
- Pricing – ensuring that pricing options are designed for the matter and the client's objectives and that whatever the firm is proposing in terms of a pricing proposal; the firm should be prepared to

demonstrate how the cost estimate can save the client money and provide value to the client; and

- Validating the math – the firm should also be prepared to explain to the client how the firm developed its position on the cost estimate. If a client asks for an explanation or to see "the math", firms should be prepared to respond without hesitation. If done properly the firm's cost estimate will provide both clarity and assurance for the client. In the end the firm's objective on the cost estimate is to deliver fair pricing, value, and a comprehensive approach to managing a client's matter.

All factors must be understood in the due diligence process, ensuring that the cost estimate includes value indicators and the client understands their objective. Despite all of this, some clients may find it a challenge and will struggle with implementing such a strategy.

Implementing a cost estimate strategy can be as simple as utilizing a basic cost or budget template and making a determination after the client receives it as to whether the proposed price is reasonable. Or, the strategy can be complicated, including multiple criteria as part of the cost estimate plan to manage the matter. Successful cost estimate strategies have tried to maintain as little work effort as possible for both the client and the firm, but also include the right information to allow both parties to make the right decision with regard to the proposed cost estimate.

Lastly, regardless of complexity, cost estimate strategies should be simple in structure yet provide enough detail so as to be valuable to the client and worth the work effort. The strategy should also be easy to operationalize, monitor, and flexible to change.

## Working through differences on a cost estimate

It is not uncommon for a client and external counsel to differ on the quantity of time estimated by a law firm to complete a specific task or an engagement. This difference of opinion may be rooted in how each party to the cost estimate approaches risk. For example, clients may view a matter or task as being straightforward, with minimal risk, and consequently expect a law firm to assign a lower quantity of time against the task or matter. Conversely, a law firm may view the same matter or task as something that requires extra caution because of potential risk, thereby requiring more work and, hence, a higher time allotment.

To help mitigate a difference of opinion regarding quantifying an accurate amount of time a firm should spend on a task, I would encourage clients to be as prescriptive as possible in describing a task or defining significant milestones on their matters. From the client's perspective, a law firm needs to be uninhibited in its approach to cost estimates and not worry about seeking clarification from a client, especially during the engagement or cost estimate phase. Nothing sours a relationship more than surprise overages on agreed-upon cost estimates because a firm failed to seek clarity on the scope of engagement or a task or made false and costly assumptions.

Clients need to ensure that they communicate their scope clearly and identify and define expectations at the time of engagement and not assume that a firm will intuitively understand the client's instructions, especially when those instructions are less than satisfactory or plagued with ambiguity. In these types of scenarios, I would encourage firms to speak up and not be shy about approaching clients for clarification or to point out ambiguities in the scope of a matter. This is particularly true for firms that enjoy being on a client's panel and are privileged to be considered designated counsel.

I have often witnessed situations where clients have increasingly become lackadaisical with regards to their own compliance processes such as defining scope or tasks on a new matter when engaging their panel firms. Over time, some clients get accustomed to utilizing the same panel firms and build up a familiarity with the professionals in the firm. Familiarity can easily lead a client to become complacent, take shortcuts and make assumptions such as a firm will understand a client's instructions even though they may be poorly written, plagued with ambiguity, or even describe the legal issue inadequately. That is why both parties to the cost estimate should look to discuss the variables of a matter or task to better understand each other's approach and/or perspective. Leaning on a law firm's expertise and experience (with other clients) in such circumstances can be invaluable as a variety of factors, unbeknownst to the client, may ultimately impact a matter and consequently the cost. Clients who may be presumptuously suspicious of a firm's motivation for wanting to undertake additional work, or change the scope partway through a matter, should first try to understand the issue before making assumptions about a firm's motivation. Not everything in the law is motivated by profit. Firms have a genuine desire to do the best job they can for a client. They want to build a relationship. Very few are in it for a one-time transaction. They want to be there for the client for the long haul. Once again, the importance of communication cannot be understated, especially in a scenario where there can be a difference of opinion, suspicion, or lack of understanding on the part of one party.

Changes in the law, market events, new regulatory requirements or experiences with other law firm clients are just a few unforeseen factors that can have an impact on a client's budget or may impact the scope of the legal work that a law firm undertakes for a client.

Whether a client is dealing with a panel firm or a new firm, the goal of in-house counsel or legal ops should be to achieve a mutual and clear understanding of the matter, legal issues, scope of engagement (what to do and not to do), clear expectations, timelines and understanding what, if any, variables need to be included or excluded from the cost estimate.

## Educating lawyers on the business of law

Lawyers traditionally are educated on the law and not the business of law. So it comes as no surprise that many lawyers (in-house and externally at firms) are neophytes when it comes to understanding the mechanics of cost estimates, budgeting, or project management practices.

I have encountered many situations, in the past and to this day, where lawyers are not familiar with how to develop a budget or how to manage a protracted matter using LPM practices. Changes in the legal marketplace and client demands are requiring that lawyers today become more business-focused and develop some level of business knowledge (i.e. understanding around basic accounting and budgeting principles) so as to be prepared to understand and assist their clients with their needs and requirements.

It is important for law firms today to proactively train their staff on business knowledge and ensure that their staff are empowered with the proper skillset, tools, and business knowledge to assist existing and future clients with their business as well as legal needs. Having the proper business knowledge around cost estimates allows a lawyer to have a meaningful and strategic dialogue with their client. Clients expect this from law firms as there is an assumption in the marketplace that many firms today will be conversant in basic accounting and have an understanding of cost estimate practices. I believe it is a necessary requirement if a firm is to stay competitive. Understanding the business of law, delivery, and how those services are to be competitively priced should be part of every firm's business strategy. Educating and training lawyers on the fundamentals of how budgets and cost estimates are developed is a needed prerequisite in today's legal marketplace and especially for those clients that are driven by data and expect the same from their law firms.

## Leveraging legal operation specialists

Many corporate legal departments have invested in legal operations subject matter experts (SMEs) and specialized legal operations (legal ops) experts who possess a unique skill set that combines project management, finance, risk, and business outsourcing expertise. Unlike internal legal business managers, legal ops are focused strictly on all things external, including the management and sourcing of external counsel.

The importance of legal ops as they relate to cost estimates cannot be understated as they bring a multitude of analytical experience and negotiating skills to the table.

Legal ops can leverage a plethora of legal e-billing data, analytics, and historical spend data that typically resides only within the corporate legal department. Legal spend data is fairly unique in its detail, and distinguishable from other, more generic, vendor billing data that is gleaned from most generic travel and expense systems found at many corporate procurement departments. Having the skill set to understand billing data nuances, patterns, and matter or practice group specifics, coupled with bespoke legal ops experience, adds value to understanding and negotiating law firms' cost estimates.

For this reason, legal ops are invaluable to internal lawyers looking to validate cost estimates that are presented to in-house counsel or internal business partners throughout a large company.

## Why do in-house counsel fail at cost estimates?

In the earlier chapter on why cost estimates fail, I identified how in-house counsel sometimes become an impediment to implementing a successful cost estimate strategy by refusing to utilize cost estimates. This has become a recurring issue for law departments at many different companies. Therefore, I thought it would be of benefit to unpack this issue to understand why this is occurring and to propose various options for clients, as well as law firms, to consider in order to help them overcome such challenges.

## Lack of executive or general counsel buy-in

Earlier I spoke about the importance of executive leadership and how "buy-in" and executive acceptance and support for any strategy or project is vital to the successful implementation of that strategy. Lawyers are programmed to follow the rules. If the general counsel announces a requirement or new policy, most lawyers will comply unequivocally without fail. However, if the GC does not support an initiative and its process and utilization is left to self-manage with very little oversight, the initiative will struggle and have limited or no success at all.

GCs cannot manage by simple decrees. Highly intelligent professionals such as lawyers and clerks will benefit more by having a value proposition put in front of them. Showing folks why cost estimates need to be implemented and the derived benefit from them helps create greater acceptance, which can lead to greater utilization and participation in the strategy. If people can identify with the objective on a more personal level that also helps to achieve greater utilization. Having some sort of governance structure in place to oversee the success and participation rate of constituents helps move things along as well as identify pockets or groups of folks that are either unwilling or simply can't find the time.

## The impact of time constraints

Lawyers have struggled with cost estimates for a variety of reasons. One of the most recurring, almost thematic, reasons is because in-house counsel just simply cannot find the time to dedicate to cost estimates. For many in-house counsel at large corporations, it's an uphill battle just keeping on top of multiple and competing matters right out of the gate every morning. I have seen this at several large companies that I have worked for where in-house legal teams struggle to stay afloat with massive workloads as a result of corporate cutbacks and finite resources and having to do more with less. Finite resources and time, coupled with all of the other responsibilities such as managing other staff, dealing with multiple internal business clients, reviewing and authorizing legal bills, non-stop meetings and conference calls (the list goes on) leaves a constituency of in-house counsel wanting less administration and not more. For this group who don't have the time, implementing cost estimates is viewed as another burden or simply another administrative chore, regardless of the cost benefits.

Faced with a multitude of internal challenges, it's no wonder cost estimates have been relegated to the back of the line in terms of priorities for many legal departments. I have seen many lawyers who are taxed for time and resources simply delegate cost estimate responsibilities to junior clerks or administrative assistants in their department. Not exactly the best approach, but it may work if the in-house lawyer commits to checking in once in a while to oversee the progress and status of cost estimates (see next section below).

For those lawyers who can't find time, perhaps they can review their responsibilities and see if cost estimates can be made a priority for them to manage. Perhaps it may mean a similar solution as delegating other responsibilities to other professionals to make room for cost estimates. If a company has selected a specific dollar threshold or practice area for cost estimates to be implemented, the workload may not be as heavy as some may think.

### Dealing with lack of support

My experience at a variety of companies has taught me that people will always want to take a shortcut and bypass any administration if they feel the process is without any value. I have heard lawyers comment that they didn't go to law school in order to complete and validate templates. It is undeniable that the study of law focuses very little on the business of law or the economics around profitability or cost savings. What is also true is that the legal market has changed and continues to change due to market competition, digitization, AI, and a myriad of other client-driven initiatives like cost estimate requirements. Clients are the buyers of legal services in a very competitive environment. Internal lawyers, as well as internal business clients, that question the value of cost estimates or dismiss them as an administrative burden, may be undermining their GC and their company's strategic goals around sustained profitability and controlling company expenses.

I believe that most lawyers today understand the value proposition and the importance of controlling external legal costs. I don't think there is a major corporation in the marketplace that relies on external counsel where the in-house legal team isn't concerned about controlling their legal costs. Almost every large corporate in-house legal team has a focus on understanding their external legal expenses and trying to figure out better ways of reducing those expenses. Anyone paying a legal bill should understand the value of a well thought-out cost estimate.

Any implementation plan always needs to understand how a strategy will impact its constituents. If lawyers don't think that cost estimates are worth the time, then it's highly unlikely that they will be extra disciplined to find the time to utilize them.

I once assisted a client in implementing a cost estimate strategy in a very challenging business environment. Although the general counsel saw merit and value in having a cost estimate strategy, many of his staff resisted its implementation and saw it as an unnecessary chore and burden. After lukewarm acceptance we chose other professionals in the legal department and some internal business managers to be responsible for managing the oversight and working individually with lawyers and business executives whenever they needed to implement a cost estimate on a significant matter. This small group of professionals interacted with in-house counsel as needed, assumed much of the workload (thereby liberating the lawyers' time) and also worked with their business counterparts and external counsel to make the initiative extremely successful to the organization.

### Lawyers are business neophytes

Over the years many lawyers have confided in me about their discomfort with business practices, project management, and accounting principles, including simple math – in short, they hate doing cost estimates. Lawyers were trained in the law and were not expected to be accountants. Many lawyers are neophytes when it comes to understanding basic accounting principles. Consequently, very few lawyers are entirely comfortable with having to deal with cost estimate or budget proposals. This point was made alarmingly clear to me when, years ago, I asked a seasoned lawyer what he thought of Excel. He said he had never stayed there. I quickly realized he thought I was referring to a hotel in Las Vegas. Although humorous, his response was not particularly shocking to me as I have come across many lawyers who don't understand, nor do they want anything to do with, the financial side of legal services unless it directly impacts their compensation. As one lawyer told me once, "accounting practices, budgeting or simply anything and everything having to do with math is left to our finance folks".

### Training lawyers on the business of law

The solution for this imperfection (and possibly a superiority complex for some lawyers) is simple; basic budget and accounting training. Many companies today conduct basic internal training sessions for legal staff to bring greater awareness to the importance of understanding the basics when it comes to pricing legal work, AFAs, and how to utilize budgets and cost estimate templates. When lawyers take the time to educate themselves on some of the basic budget principles such as cost estimate templates, mathematical averages, medians, AFAs, understanding and calculating staffing ratios and even basic familiarity with Excel, all of these things no longer seem foreign (or intimidating) to them as they gain greater comfort and understanding and an appreciation for utilizing them.

Gaining familiarity with basic accounting concepts is not overly difficult and can be learned relatively easily. What in-house counsel also struggle with is any activity or business process that adds more administration to their existing processes or looks to change their processes and may require new learning. I have touched on this in the preceding paragraphs, but how clients operationalize a cost estimate strategy is critically important. Each client must review their internal processes and ensure that the cost estimate strategy they are implementing will work within their department or organization. Successful deployment of a cost estimate strategy or the implementation of simple budget templates will only work if the users buy-in to a process that is straightforward and easy to use and they see value in the process. What may work at one company may not work at another.

## A simplified cost estimate process ensures success

Moreover, if the cost estimate or budget template can be designed as a smart form (definition) or can have simple array formulas embedded to automatically do simple mathematical calculations, this makes it even simpler for lawyers and business folks to deal with the cost estimates that are returned to them. Making the cost estimate as simple and straightforward as possible helps ensure greater acceptance and buy-in by those folks who have to use the cost tools.

Automation is being utilized with greater frequency by corporate clients as many software systems can accommodate customized cost estimate or budgeting templates, specific to a matter or a practice area.

Regardless of how simplified a legal ops team can make the cost estimate template, lawyers may still see it as a low priority and sometimes conveniently forget to ask for it on their next matter. In a decentralized environment where internal business clients can engage law firms without the consent of the legal department, there is a greater risk of businesses not following established protocols. Business clients may not share the same zeal for tracking legal costs that the legal department does. This is exactly why support from the GC's office or senior executives is needed as well as some type of compliance monitoring where in-house counsel and business clients know that their participation is being monitored and failure to comply may have some sort of consequences. Moreover, law firms can help in-house legal teams with monitoring and ensuring business group compliance with cost estimate strategies as the firm plays a key role in ensuring that they complete a cost estimate proposal, regardless if the client asked for one. This is again especially important in a decentralized environment where clients may not be able to ensure 100 percent compliance with established cost estimate processes. Most firms will comply with whatever direction they receive from a GC. Cost estimates can be made a mandatory process and attached to a client's terms of engagement. If a business client or in-house lawyer fails to request that a firm complete a cost estimate, most certainly the law firm will not forget if it is a requirement and part of their terms of engagement.

## The trust factor

Many in-house lawyers work at a law firm prior to making the move in-house. These lawyers are very familiar with the established processes at a firm for working on client matters. They may also have worked alongside many different types of staff before moving into a corporate legal environment. It is therefore understandable that many in-house lawyers have a longstanding (trusting) friendship with many of the lawyers that they once worked alongside and now have to utilize for assistance on internal corporate matters.

Therefore in-house lawyers (i.e. clients) may be extremely trusting of their external counterparts, so much so that they forgo the need for a cost estimate on the understanding that they as the client are getting a good deal from their old firm. In this type of scenario, trust replaces the need for any tool to verify the firm's cost proposal. I have seen this type of scenario play out repeatedly over the years, where in-house counsel has blatantly bypassed the need to validate a firm's proposal and trust what the firm delivers as absolute. Clients should trust their firms to provide them with the most reasonable cost proposals. However, part of that proposal or quote should be a validation process in the form of a cost estimate that provides an additional level of validation that trust on its own cannot provide.

## What law firms dislike most about cost estimates

Many firms realize the importance that cost estimates play in their relationship with many corporate legal departments. Providing accurate and meaningful data and how a firm intends to manage a matter is invaluable to the client. Firms understand this, but are frustrated at times because of impediments that make their job more difficult. I have heard firms repeatedly lament to me about how frustrated they are with in-house counsel or business folks who cannot manage a matter after they have agreed to a mutual cost estimate. As one firm told me, "We are not clairvoyant, if they (the client) change up the scope and have different expectations around what they need, they need to tell us. We get beat up when we make assumptions and are almost always asked to eat legitimate costs. Sometimes we feel like we are being taken advantage of."

I am sure many firms can relate to this comment and have had similar experiences. As many will also confess, the utilization of cost estimates with clients is far from perfect.

Figure 8 shows a top ten list of challenges that law firms lament about in trying to work through cost estimates with their clients.

| | TOP TEN LIST OF LAW FIRM CHALLENGES |
|---|---|
| 1 | Poorly defined scope |
| 2 | Scope change |
| 3 | Poor communication and access to client |
| 4 | No central point of contact |
| 5 | Forced write down of overages |
| 6 | Delays in authorizing cost estimates |
| 7 | Clients' refusal to negotiate |
| 8 | Cost estimate is overly complicated |
| 9 | Cost estimate is a moving target |
| 10 | Client doesn't know what they want in regards to cost estimate |

*Figure 8: Top ten challenges law firms face.*

## Poorly defined scope

Suboptimal scope definition, including how a client defines its business requirements, project, or legal requirements is a huge impediment from the outset and handicaps the firm's ability to make a proper cost assessment and deliver an accurate cost estimate to the client. Many times, firms are left with having to increase their costs in order to cover off variables and assumptions that have not been clearly identified or defined in a poorly written scope narrative. This presents challenges later when firms are challenged by clients on overages.

## Scope change

Similar to poorly defined scope, changes to scope in some circumstances (litigation, negotiations) are uncontrollable and may be honestly unexpected. But, more often, scope can change because the client neglected to consider variables, or did not conduct a proper assessment of the matter before engaging the firm.

Changes to scope partway through a matter may impact multiple factors that will certainly impact price if the scope requires additional work and resources. Additional work ordinarily is welcome at any firm, but clients are not always receptive to understanding that the cost for services needs to change as well. If the firm uncovers an unforeseen legal issue that requires additional work or altering the scope of a matter, then again a revision and recalibration of the original cost estimate is required.

Ensuring that thorough discussions take place prior to any engagement ensures that all parties understand the ground rules around how any recalibration will take place, when, how, and who will be notified.

### Poor communication and access to client

Many firms will tell you that clients regularly drop the ball when it comes to issuing clear and accurate instructions on an engagement or what they expect on a cost estimate. Moreover, there is still room for improvement, training, and education on the topic of cost estimates with in-house counsel and their internal business folks as firms feel many clients lack familiarity and comfort with using cost estimates.

Often instructions lack clarity or are ambiguous and not as definitive as the firm would like. Cost estimate discussions need to improve and clients need to appreciate that a law firm cannot regularly write down their legal costs because of the client's inability to communicate.

Law firms should consider a more direct and proactive approach when it comes to communication. They should worry less about risking that they might offend or bother the client and directly approach the client whenever they have questions or concerns. Seeking clarity on engagement instructions should never be brushed off. I have seen all too often how firms have made costly assumptions, instead of contacting the client and seeking a clarification.

### No central point of contact

This seems to be a very simple and straightforward issue. Clients need to ensure that they have assigned a professional who is responsible for the cost estimate as well as the matter and that the professional is the point person for any questions or concerns and for advising the firm of any changes to the cost estimate or matter.

Firms complain that in-house counsel at large companies often hand the matter and the firm over to internal business clients after a cost estimate has been agreed upon. Many times the law firm is not familiar with their internal business folks' processes or expectations and the firm is left on its own and has to rely on the cost estimate elements for direction.

This gets even more complicated when firms need clarification or have questions that only in-house counsel can answer but they are difficult to reach. Consequently, business clients get frustrated at unexpected delays that are caused by firms not being able to get answers from the client's side. What can appear as a simple administrative issue can over a short period escalate into multiple areas of concern that ultimately impact the work effort and potentially the reputation of the law firm. In-house counsel understand the law and may be more sympathetic to a delay caused by an unexpected legal issue; however, business clients who are seldom experts on the law may be less understanding and consequently forgiving.

Furthermore, if the matter involves multiple points of contact at the client's company, this may further complicate things as a firm may receive conflicting instructions that impact the outcome of the matter. Clients should be responsible for ensuring that their firms have one primary professional to contact – with a backup if need be.

For situations where in-house counsel are understaffed or lack the time to manage a matter, they should consider delegating the responsibility to another member of their team such as a senior clerk or a project manager who can take on the responsibility of overseeing the matter and fielding questions. This same contact person may also be responsible for managing any pricing and/or changes to the cost estimate or scope if required.

Assigning a point of contact or responsible professional, providing a warm hand-off to business folks, as well as creating an alternative contact on black swan events, all help to mitigate delays on a matter and to keep costs down as firms don't have to make costly assumptions because the right folks cannot be contacted.

### Forced write down of overages

Clients don't like surprises, especially unexpected overages. If the cost estimate has not addressed this point, firms are usually at the mercy of their clients and, more often than not, are asked to write down any overages because the client will not pay them.

Where firms get especially frustrated is when the extra work that resulted in the overage is of value to the client. It could have been caused by an unexpected variance, change in scope, or maybe even the client's fault in poorly defined business requirements. Regardless of the circumstances, some clients are simply unyielding and will not even meet a firm halfway. They will insist it is the firm's responsibility (or fault) and require the firm to absorb the entire overage.

Firms understand the dynamics of the marketplace and how buyers use their purchasing power now as leverage whenever they want. Doing what the client asks is usually in the firm's best (financial) interest. Most firms go along with their clients' wishes so as not to jeopardize their standing with the client. However, some clients need to reevaluate their strategies around how they treat their firms with regards to overages that are legitimate. Greater consideration, and understanding, should be given especially when the unexpected work effort is of value to the client. In such circumstances, clients need to be more appreciative and extend leniency and absorb the overage as an exception.

Fortunately, most GCs that I have encountered have been extremely fair with their firms in how they have dealt with overages. GCs (many of whom have also worked at law firms) understand the economic impact a large overage can have on a firm's bottom line. Thankfully, many GCs review each matter and circumstance before making a decision. If there are reasonable circumstances that can explain the overage and why a firm proceeded to do the extra work, then most GCs are accommodating and will allow some leniency in making an exception and covering the extra cost.

If internal budget constraints are the principal impediment for a client not being able to pay a firm for an unexpected overage, then perhaps, in all fairness to the firm, the client should consider and explore all opportunities to try to adjust its budget and make some sort of accommodation to cover the cost. Exceptions can always be made if the right reasons and explanation is put forward.

Lastly, I believe that firms need to assert themselves better in the face of forced write-downs attributable to overages – especially if the firm is not at fault. Managing partners at panel firms should take the lead and remind their clients of the impact that the write downs have on the firm's revenue stream and ultimately the compensation of individuals at that firm. Quite simply, if the work completed by a firm was legitimate and of value to the client, firms should not back down on being paid. Reasonable and fair clients will not act punitively and seek to take advantage of a firm by requiring a write down, especially if the work product was of value to the client.

One way of reminding clients of a firm's sacrifice may be to create a "value services report" that can highlight all of the work that the firm completed for the client in a given period of time. Included in this report would be the matters where the firm absorbed overages on behalf of the client. Firms might want to include such items as the total time and dollar value of their write downs and perhaps even break out the write downs by individual matters if there were multiple write down requests over a certain period of time.

Providing a value services report that includes write downs is a subtle way of demonstrating the extent of a firm's commitment to their relationship with the client. It's not uncommon for clients to lose track of how many times they have requested firms to write down legal costs. Most internal legal departments with panels of firms, sometimes a few hundred firms, don't typically track write downs.

Smart clients may honestly forget the extent or frequency they ask their firms to write down, especially if they have hundreds of matters with a multitude of firms. A simple report may also serve as a subtle notice for clients to improve their engagement processes, specifically around how they provide instructions to external counsel and define their requirements around their engagements. Such improvements may help mitigate the incidents of overages occurring and firms having to write off unnecessary legal costs because of the client.

### Delays in authorizing cost estimates

I have seen many circumstances where legal work needed to be done ASAP and the panel firm was engaged by in-house counsel without any discussion around pricing. I am not quite sure who is more to blame for this circumstance, but both parties end up, down the road, in an uncomfortable discussion about writing down work that the client thought was unnecessary or questioning the staffing ratio or the quantity of time a certain timekeeper spent on a particular task – the list goes on. In-house counsel dislike administration. Having to complete cost templates seems like a burden to some. It's not surprising that many lawyers still bypass what they consider an administrative chore and default to hourly rates. Sometimes it's easier and they look to trust their firm – until the first bill arrives.

Many clients will tell you that they need special permission from their GC or a business executive to approve a budget or cost estimate proposal, but that they still want the firm to start work on the matter while they wait for the approval. Firms are put in a difficult position. If they are lucky to be on a panel, then they assume the client will not stiff them and ultimately honor the cost estimate proposal – whenever they get around to it. However, this leap of faith only goes so far as many firms can attest that many clients may end up revising and lowering proposals, even after a great deal of the work has been done.

Ideally, the simple answer to this dilemma is not to start work without an approved cost estimate. Practically though, most panel firms will tell you that not starting work until the cost estimate arrives is not how it works. Trust the client to honor the arrangement but expect that it might not be 100 percent paid in the end. It all depends on the client, relationship, company, or even the GC.

### Clients' refusal to negotiate

Not all cost estimates are simple. Complicated matters may require a cost estimate with several detailed components tied to pricing as well as instructions or requirements around variances or assumptions. I believe that most firms going into a cost estimate proposal expect to at some point negotiate some part of the cost estimate that they propose to a client. This has been the normal expectation up until the past few years where there is now an increasing resistance by some GCs and their in-house legal teams to negotiate. In fact, with an increased focus on cost containment, bigger corporate clients are unyielding when it comes to budgets. Clients will tell a firm right at the outset what they expect to pay for a matter – take it or leave it. The client does not want to negotiate. This "take it or leave it" type strategy may seem somewhat heavy handed and unfair to firms, but clients in today's marketplace have the benefit of purchasing power. They control the market and are not afraid of wielding their influence to their advantage.

I have seen more and more companies adopting a "take it or leave it" strategy, especially with regard to transactional or commoditized legal work. Right or wrong, clients know (either from data analysis or experience) what they expect to pay for certain services. They may understand, better than any firm, the value of particular legal work within their company. All the data that a law firm has won't change a client's thinking. The client knows what it has been paying (historically) and what it wants to pay going forward. At some point in a cost estimate process both parties have to agree but for some clients that may appear abrupt and unyielding to the firm. In the end the firm has to decide whether or not the cost or budget that a client is expecting is economically viable for the firm. Not everything in a cost estimate today, including price, is negotiable and clients are not shy about reminding firms of this.

**Cost estimate is overly complicated**

Some clients needlessly require firms to go through a very extensive cost estimate process when a simple solution or strategy will suffice. For simple transactional matters, clients should always consider the cost of any added administrative process against the benefits and whether firms needlessly have to comply with a multitude of data requirements when in fact only a few would be sufficient. This is especially true for transactional matters that are recurring and identical in nature with a very low risk of any variances occurring.

I have seen instances where clients have tried to gain greater control of their legal expenses by mandating that all of their matters, regardless of dollar value, practice area or complexity, required a budget or cost estimate before a firm could be engaged and begin its work. Such requirements without any limits or caveats may create a large amount of administration and upkeep for both the client and the firm, not to mention a multitude of bureaucratic impediments for both the client and the firm.

Clients need to be cognizant that the composition of a cost estimate should be congruent to the complexity of the matter. Simple transactional matters will require far less work and cost elements than would a more complicated matter. Clients should remind themselves that understanding the complexity and objectives of matters and the variables that come into play should dictate the level of information that they request from their firms and that not all matters require a cost estimate or certainly a detailed proposal if a simpler approach can be agreed upon.

### Cost estimate is a moving target

Despite all of the work that is involved in a cost estimate, some clients will not keep to the agreed mutual agreement and will want to change the scope or narrow it over time. Sometimes a firm may have already started the work on numerous legal issues, or turned down other lucrative work because of an expectation that the cost estimate that was agreed upon will deliver a certain amount of revenue.

Lost revenue impacts firms in varying degrees, and regardless of size no firm likes to have to turn down work, but sometimes capacity becomes an issue. Having clients play with scope should not be tolerated. Firms need to affirm their position at the outset of a matter and include in their cost estimates a notification that should the client pare down the scope after work has begun, the client may still be responsible for a percentage of the original cost estimate.

I have started to see this in greater frequency over the past few years as market conditions tighten for firms. Some large (global) firms and smaller litigation boutique firms have started to add compensatory (i.e. penalty) caveats to cover themselves off should a client pare down the scope of engagement after it has begun.

If a matter is complex and there is a good probability of the scope changing after a firm has started to work on a matter, this should be reflected in the original cost estimate proposal. Both parties to the cost estimate should (mutually) agree as to how and when changes to a cost estimate can occur and unilateral changes to scope or cost should not be permitted. If either party anticipates that a change needs to be made or the cost estimate needs to be recalibrated, then this should be communicated ahead of the changes occurring – this includes curtailing the scope of the engagement, expanding it by including variances or beginning work on assumptions.

### Client doesn't know what they want in regard to cost estimate

With all of the talk around legal project management and AFAs over the past few years, it's surprising to hear firms say that there are still many clients out there (business folks as well as in-house lawyers) who are not really familiar with those cost savings practices. When it comes to cost estimates, sometimes the client doesn't even know what they want. Clients may ask a firm to propose a budget or an estimate for them to get an idea around potential costs on a matter and that is all the direction the client gives a firm. It's almost as if the firm is left on its own to create something, anything for the client. This appears simple on the surface, but can later become problematic for the firm in a variety of ways.

Firms may take it upon themselves to create a thorough cost estimate proposal, investing a lot of time and resources in preparing something for the client. Without any real direction from the client, they may not like what the firm returns to them. Consequently, this leaves the firm with a dissatisfied client and the firm having wasted a lot of time and energy in creating something that is of little value. Without proper direction from the client and a thorough understanding of the scope or legal issue, firms may invariably have to rely on risky and pricey assumptions, which in and of themselves can also create dissatisfaction with clients because of a higher price tag for the firm's services. I have heard clients complain about cost estimates being too high when all along the reason they are high is because the client failed to give the firm proper direction around the scope.

If the client is engaging a law firm for services, the onus rests on the client to identify the scope of the engagement as clearly as possible. Even if the client doesn't know what to expect in a cost estimate, a good firm should be able to prepare something that is of benefit and value for the client, provided the firm has been given the proper information. Firms should resist the temptation to go away and create whatever they like without proper client direction. Firms should provide assistance to the client by having a discussion around the scope and laying out possible pricing options. Having had some level of discussion, the firm can then be guided to work on a cost estimate that can be in line with what the clients' expectations are on the matter.

### The resistance to utilize cost estimates

While the utilization of cost estimates with many corporate clients has been steadily growing, it has not come without challenges and is still far from unanimously accepted. Companies of all shapes and sizes struggle with a multitude of implementation issues as well as cultural and resource issues that either delay or prevent the successful implementation of cost estimate strategies. Some of the reasons are legitimate and tied to economic or resource constraints. Some clients just simply can't do everything they would like to and have to pick and choose between initiatives and projects that will make a real difference right away, and some that will have to be delayed. In other circumstances, the reasons tend to sound more like excuses borne out of a simple lack of understanding or desire to understand.

Perhaps the biggest obstacle that I have seen in regard to implementing cost estimates (regardless of industry) has been the lack of support (i.e. "buy-in") for a cost estimate strategy from senior executives, especially a company's GC.

Nothing undermines the credibility of an initiative more than a lack of support from senior managers. This type of behavior sends a clear and wrongful message to all employees that, whatever the initiative, it's not really important and employees don't really have to participate or comply. Unfortunately, in my career I have seen this occur all too often as the GC or his/her executive leadership has purposely and not out of circumstance failed to buy into supporting a cost estimates strategy.

There are a multitude of other reasons why either in-house counsel or internal business operations folks have failed to recognize the true and long-term value a cost estimate strategy would bring to their organization. Below are listed some of the reasons (and excuses) that I have experienced:

- Cost estimates don't create "real" quantifiable cost savings for the command, just an added administrative burden;
- In-house counsel don't have the time to be negotiating and tracking cost estimates;
- The legal department doesn't have the resources to manage a cost estimate process;
- In-house lawyers and internal business clients lack proper business acumen to successfully implement such a process;
- If we don't trust our firms on hourly rates, why would we trust them on cost estimates (this point will be discussed in greater depth later on);
- We have tried some form of cost estimates before and the firms are all over the place on feedback, which really hasn't helped;

- Firms always provide a very wide dollar range, which is not helpful;
- Cost estimates we receive are always too high and unrealistic;
- Internal business folks don't have the time (too busy) and won't buy-in to utilizing cost estimates;
- We can't monitor compliance with cost estimates, firms don't bill us what's in the cost estimate;
- Internal business clients hire firms without using cost estimates; and
- We have negotiated hourly rates so why do we need cost estimates?

It is always easier for management to find an excuse or reason to turn down something (a project, a goal) if their personal bias prevents them from recognizing its value. Managers will often utilize lack of resources or the prioritization of other more important initiatives as obstacles for implementing new strategies that they may not be familiar with. Most challenging initiatives require an investment, dedication, and desire to see it through. These criteria are ingredients for success but unfortunately may not always be readily present in all in-house legal teams.

Regardless of the reason or excuse, if company GCs cannot understand and support the potential value that cost estimate strategies may bring, then there is very little chance any real value will be derived from the client in implementing such a strategy.

Regardless of the client's reason for not implementing a cost estimate strategy, firms should not wait for clients to request a cost estimate before the firm proposes one. I believe there is a duty and responsibility on the part of all firms to be upfront and unabashedly transparent in how they price their work and propose to manage a client's matter. Moreover, cost estimates should be part of a firm's standard modus operandi and value added services strategy. Cost estimates offer firms an opportunity to demonstrate to the client, and the market, a firm's commitment to providing great legal work, excellent service delivery, and transparency in how the firm is prepared to deliver value through its pricing proposal.

**Beware of law firm caveats and disclaimers**

Generally, clients expect that the cost estimates that they receive on transactional matters will be less complicated and exclude any caveats and disclaimers that qualify the work effort that the firm expects to complete for the client.

Qualifying remarks typically tend to reaffirm a particular position or understanding a firm is taking on a matter. The firm will make these remarks in the form of a disclaimer to ensure that the client understands that the firm's work is conditional on the disclaimer. For routine or transactional matters, it is uncommon to see any disclaimers as both the client and firm understand the scope of an engagement to be pretty straightforward with the unlikely possibility that something (e.g. assumption or variance) will derail the firm's successful completion of their engagement.

On more complex matters, where there is a greater probability of a variance occurring or where the firm may have to make assumptions, firms are more likely to want to qualify their work effort by utilizing some type of disclaimer.

Clients need to pay attention to the content of these disclaimers because most often were they to be utilized on a matter, the disclaimer will directly impact the overall cost of the estimate. Disclaimers may describe how certain tasks, staffing ratios, deliverables, timelines, work effort and inevitably costs may be impacted should something occur or not occur. Disclaimers will almost always include a reference to assumptions or variances, which will also provide details around changes to the cost estimate price.

For example, if a firm encounters a certain variance, such as requiring extra time and effort and resources in negotiating with a third party, the firm may state this as a qualifier to the cost estimate that they provided where originally the client did not foresee any negotiation. Disclaimers cover off firms for the "what if something should occur" scenario.

Most clients don't mind seeing one or two disclaimers on a cost estimate as it demonstrates that the firm is giving thought to the matter and is looking out for the client in a proactive manner. Where disclaimers become problematic is when firms list multiple disclaimers and it creates confusion for the clients in understanding all of the different scenarios. I have seen some lawyers on occasion get extremely overzealous (and defensive) and want to cover off every possible scenario. This is not to anyone's benefit.

In the end a firm should ask itself whether there is a need to include more than one disclaimer. In fact, a better approach would be to discuss the possible "what if" scenarios with the client directly before recording them in the actual cost estimate. Unless the client asks for it or both parties mutually agree to adding the disclaimer, a firm should consider omitting it from the cost estimate. Having multiple disclaimers with differing cost addendums may only create confusion for the client, added work, and potentially unnecessary frustration with the firm.

I believe that a disclaimer should only be used if there is a strong likelihood of a variance occurring. Even then, the disclaimer should be clear and simple to read and track for the client. Law firms should avoid using extremely technical legal jargon as simple English will suffice.

Over the years I have seen some very complicated disclaimers that were written to be purposely vague or ambiguous or just didn't make any sense from an economic perspective. One disclaimer that stands out for its audacity and brazenness described in a footnote how a law firm expected to charge the client a premium of three percent (in addition to its mutually agreed upon fees) if the firm completed the work. This should not be confused with a risk/reward type fee arrangement. When I confronted the firm on this disclaimer and questioned what the three percent premium fee pertained to, the firm responded by stating that it was a "value tax". The firm actually thought that it could charge a fee for agreeing to deliver its services!

# Chapter 4:
# Value and cost estimates

Can a client put a price on value? The short answer is yes. The price for legal services in a cost estimate (regardless of the form that price takes) may vary depending on a variety of value indicators such as the type of matter, complexity, staffing, risk level, scope, and unexpected variances.

Clients who have graduated past the hourly billing model and AFAs have come to understand that the proposed price that appears in the cost estimate is simply the value proposition that both parties have agreed to.

Clients differ on how they go about quantifying a value proposition. For years, many clients rarely ever approached the subject of value with their firms, especially in a cost estimate discussion. If a client or a firm was progressive and did brush the topic, it was always in a bit of a convoluted discussion that lacked any real tangible way of analyzing what many still consider to be unquantifiable. Even today, many clients and firms still have a difficult time in getting their heads around determining the true value of a law firm's work. I would agree that there is still the subjective element to such an exercise, but I also think that, with a little bit of work, value can be quantified.

## Measuring value using value indicators

The value that clients place on the legal services they receive from their firms can vary depending on the importance or significance a client places on a particular matter. In some situations, such as a class action litigation matter or potential merger or acquisition, the legal services being provided are significantly more complex and of strategic importance than a simple transaction or routine matter.

The cost estimate that a client expects to receive for these two scenarios can be quite different. Regardless of practice area, complexity, or cost, it is the buyer of legal services (i.e. the client) who is the principal arbiter in determining whether or not they have received value from the cost estimate that is proposed.

The determination of value can be made either by way of an evaluation, usually involving some sort of analysis and reconciliation against the client's historical database, or by a more visceral and subjective approach. Most clients up until fairly recently have benchmarked value using a less scientific (i.e. empirical) approach as not all clients have the benefit of legal ops folks or data crunchers who can spend hours at a time slicing and dicing mountains of billing data.

Until the advent of e-billing software systems and data mining capabilities, most clients would rely on historical past experience or subjective criteria to make a determination as to whether they received value on a matter. Non empirical criteria that may have been as simple as deciding whether the firm solved their legal issue or mitigated risk for the client were primarily atop the value list. As clients started to be exposed to greater quantities of data, value became something that could be quantified, measured, benchmarked, and tracked. Despite advances in data tracking and monitoring, clients continue to rely on subjective criteria to help them define whether or not they have received value from their firms. I refer to the subjective criteria that a client uses as "value indicators".

Value indicators are similar to performance or delivery indicators that clients typically use to measure a law firm's service level performance. Value indicators, from a cost estimate scenario, ultimately help the client to understand (and measure) whether what the firm is proposing is of any value to the client. Value indicators are focused mostly on service delivery, matter management, and the cost of a matter, as opposed to the quality of the legal advice being provided by a firm.

Below are listed a few value indicators, along with some actionable questions for clients to consider.

- Staffing ratio – is how the firm proposes to staff the matter adequate or is the firm proposing to over staff the matter? Is the client familiar with the professionals that will be working on the matter or is the firm staffing junior professionals with limited experience? Is the client comfortable with the staffing ratio and that the professionals have the right level of experience to provide value to the matter?
- Cost and type of pricing arrangement – does the pricing proposal makes sense given the nature of the matter. Are there any hidden or baked-in costs to cover off assumptions that the firm has made? If so, should these be removed? Is the cost estimate in line with previous historical data the client might have? If not, can the client live with the delta between their numbers and the firm's or is further discussion required?

- Scope definition – are all parties to the matter (including a client's internal business partners) in mutual agreement on how the scope is defined? Are there any areas of ambiguity?
- Assumptions – is it clear to all parties that there are to be no assumptions? If assumptions are required, has the firm provided an adequate explanation around the assumptions and their respective costs? Is the client comfortable with the additional costs, should the assumptions be required? Has the firm proposed a plan to deal with assumptions and notification to the client should the firm need to utilize an assumption scenario?
- Overages – how will excess costs be dealt with? Is there a plan in place to contact the client ahead of the overage? Who will be responsible for overages if the client is not contacted?
- Communication plan – is there an adequate communication plan in place with responsible professionals identified and a back-up support contact identified? At what point in the matter does the client expect to be contacted? Does the firm know when it is to contact the client? Who can renegotiate the cost estimate if it is required? Can the law firm continue to perform its work while a cost estimate is being revised?
- WIP notification – if the matter is significant, is there a plan in place to contact and advise the client when the firm has met a particular dollar threshold as it is working through a matter? Do both parties understand what the dollar threshold is? What happens if the dollar threshold is exceeded without the client's consent?

As mentioned earlier, most of the value indicators are not quantifiable criteria. However, value indicators can be rated empirically, tracked, and monitored so as to help a client make a determination whether or not they have received value in regard to such things as monitoring the progress of a budget, staffing resources against a matter, defining scope, or how a firm manages the variances or assumptions on a matter.

Clients should ensure that they understand the whole picture around a cost estimate and not merely focus on the pricing component. Whether or not a firm can deliver on its cost estimate is dependent on a multitude of value indicators. How the firm proposes to manage the different elements of a matter (e.g. value indicators) will determine client satisfaction with the cost estimate and whether or not the client has received true value on the matter.

Lastly, both clients and firms need to ensure that they have a mutual discussion upfront at the time of engagement, especially on extraordinary matters, around the subject of value. If a client hasn't asked the firm about its value proposition, then a firm should highlight this in its cost estimate discussion. Clients may make certain assumptions of how services will be delivered. It doesn't hurt to emphasize the value indicators as it can only give the client greater assurance in knowing that it has selected the right firm for its engagement.

## Value indicators

I believe that the best way to measure whether value has been derived on a matter, or in a relationship, with a firm is by using value indicators specific to legal services. Below are listed what I believe to be some of the most important common value indicators:

- Quality of legal advice (expertise/knowledge);
- Timeliness/responsiveness;
- Staffing of matter (staff utilization ratio of partners vs associates and others);
- Communication (clear, responsive, proactive – asks questions);
- Price (structure and affordability);
- Service delivery (customer service);
- Commitment (makes you feel like you are the only client);
- Risk mitigation (reputation or legal);
- Trust (assurance, reliability);
- Technology (leverages IT for the benefit of the matter);
- KM, LPM, practices;
- Efficiency;
- Cost savings (can they show us they saved us money?);
- Institutional knowledge (do they know our business / share our beliefs?);
- Complexity of matter; and
- Cost estimate response.

I believe that value can be measured by using value indicators. Although they may have a price component, they can be grouped to create a framework by which value is delivered to the client. I think that there has been a common misconception in the marketplace for years, amongst both clients and firms, that the value of a matter can be tabulated by adding up the total balance of invoices on a matter. Unfortunately, that is not true. Cost should never be confused with value. The true value of a cost estimate is therefore not measured by empirical elements but by a mutually agreed upon set of value indicators that, if achieved successfully, deliver value to the client. In exchange for that success the client compensates the firm by paying the price established (up front) in the cost estimate with the firm. Without the value discussion, one cannot guarantee that value will be derived from the engagement, or that both parties will hold each other accountable to the mutually agreed cost estimate.

Value indicators provide the added benefit of knowing what the expectations are on a matter or in a relationship. They provide transparency into understanding what criteria the client sees as being important and valuable. Without defined value indicators, firms are left to guess or make assumptions as to what other criteria in a cost estimate arrangement (next to price) is important. Worse yet, firms run the risk of minimizing or outright dismissing some indicators as not important.

Therefore, the price in a cost estimate is determined by the value a client places on the final work effort. That effort is made up of value indicators to be delivered by the firm. If a firm successfully meets the client's expectations, there is a high likelihood that the client will realize value from the services provided.

It is integral to the success of any matter that the client and firm have a discussion upfront before any work commences and that they mutually agree upon the specific value indicators and how value will be determined at the beginning of the matter. Whether the final pricing arrangement in the cost estimate is based on hourly rates, flat or fixed fees, tasked-based or some other type of AFA or risk reward arrangement, the client will make the final determination as to whether or not it is satisfied with the work effort and therefore whether value was delivered on the matter.

### Law firm value indicator calculator

For clients looking for a more analytical and quantifiable approach to track value on a matter or in a relationship with a firm, I have created a law firm value indicator calculator form (Figure 9) to help with measuring and tracking the value they have received from a firm.

The value indicator form is comprised of 15 value indicators that clients can use to quantify and rate a firm after a matter has been completed. I would suggest that each value indicator be assigned an empirical weighting. The weighting should be based on the importance that each value indicator has to either a specific matter or the overall relationship between the firm and the client. Summing up the total of all of the value indicators will produce a score that can then be compared against an evaluation scale measuring Low, Medium, and High to identify what level of value the client has received from the firm. Sharing the calculator form as part of a cost estimate discussion in advance of work being completed provides transparency to the relationship and also helps the firm to understand which value indicators the client finds most attractive to its company.

| **Law Firm Value Indicator Calculator** | | **Rating score card** | | | |
|---|---|---|---|---|---|
| | **Value indicators** | **High (5)** | **Medium (3)** | **Low (1)** | **N/A** |
| 1 | Quality of legal advice (expertise/knowledge) | O | O | O | O |
| 2 | Responsiveness (meets deadlines, answers questions, follows up, proactive) | O | O | O | O |
| 3 | Staffing of matter (staff utilization ratio of professionals is equitable) | O | O | O | O |
| 4 | Communication (clear, responsive, proactive, asks questions) | O | O | O | O |
| 5 | Price (cost structure is reasonable and affordable) | O | O | O | O |
| 6 | Commitment (focuses attention on client) | O | O | O | O |
| 7 | Risk mitigation (understands reputational and legal risk) | O | O | O | O |
| 8 | Trust (demonstrates assurance, reliability) | O | O | O | O |
| 9 | Technology (leverage IT for benefit of client) | O | O | O | O |
| 10 | Innovative KM (recycles previous work product, utilizes LPM practices) | O | O | O | O |
| 11 | Service delivery (ensures excellence in servicing client) | O | O | O | O |
| 12 | Cost savings and efficiency (demonstrates transparency re. saving client money) | O | O | O | O |
| 13 | Institutional knowledge (understands clients business, strategies, and beliefs) | O | O | O | O |
| 14 | Complexity of matter | O | O | O | O |

| **Value Indicator Calculator** | **Total Score/70** |
|---|---|
| **High Value** | **(61-70)** |
| **Medium Value** | **(40-60)** |
| **Low Value** | **(0-39)** |

*Figure 9: Law firm value indicator calculator.*

## What happens in the absence of value?

It is a highly competitive marketplace for many firms and alternative legal service providers. Firms have to be all things to all clients. Consequently, it's not uncommon to find firms that have not measured up to client expectations or have fallen short in terms of their value indicators. What happens when a client thinks it hasn't received value?

As many firms can attest, clients are not shy about letting a firm know when they think they haven't received value. In these types of situations, firms will have to choose between either agreeing with the client's assessment of their suboptimal performance or stand their ground and affirm their confidence in the work that they have done.

All too often I have seen firms acquiescing to a client's belief that the firm has fallen short on expectations (i.e. failed to provide value). This capitulation is mostly motivated by economic reasons where the firm either voluntarily or forcibly reduces a portion of its fees to satisfy the client.

In my experience, clients have not hesitated in leveraging their position in order to take advantage of firm write-downs whenever possible. Unfortunately in some circumstances I have seen a few clients use their leverage almost mercilessly and punitively without any regard for fairness or intent to meet a firm halfway on covering an overage or a write-off by the firm. Explanations like "We feel your costs don't justify the value we have received" do nothing but leave a firm stumped and with very little recourse but to fold and agree with the client. The firm also hopes that the sacrifice it has made by cutting its costs won't further impact either their status on a panel or ability to receive future work.

Ensuring that the cost estimate discussion, at the outset of matter, includes a discussion around value helps to avoid an uncomfortable situation for both the client and the firm. There is nothing worse than for a firm to have its credibility questioned. Having a discussion around value and defining expectations in a formalized cost estimate proposal helps to mitigate the risk that a firm's credibility will be called into question.

It's highly unlikely that any firm starts an engagement with its client thinking that it will fail and have to write-down a substantial portion of its work. Why would it? Failure from the outset is not even an option – if it were the client wouldn't tolerate it and would probably not hire the firm. Part of every value proposition discussion should include things like commitment, assurance, and trust in order to ensure that the work product delivered by a firm meets with the client's expectations. I have yet to see a failure clause written into a client's or firm's letter of engagement. No one ever talks about failure or has a "Were we to ever let you down" clause written into their engagement letter. This never happens, nor should it.

## Law firms need to stand their ground – clients are not always right

Lastly, the client is not always right. Sometimes the client gets it wrong. In those situations when a firm knows it is unequivocally right, and it has delivered value, the decision to hold its ground and confront the client in order to reaffirm its position becomes a very challenging one.

Challenging a client is a bold move and should not be taken lightly. However, if a firm has a longstanding historical relationship and suddenly there is a question of value, chances are pretty good that it's not about the work product but may be about service delivery, communication, timelines, or any other number of items.

If the original cost estimate discussion also included a discussion around value and indicators that set expectations for both the client and firm, I would certainly encourage firms to push back if they think they have delivered on those expectations.

In the end, there is a good chance that fault may lie with the client and not the firm. It is not uncommon for in-house counsel or their internal business partners to mismanage a matter, miscommunicate instructions, or underestimate a cost estimate or budget. All of these scenarios and many others may impact a matter or have unexpected consequences on how legal services are delivered or the outcome of a matter. Firms should not be held at fault for any extenuating circumstances that may have impacted any number of value indicators if the impact to those indicators was truly unexpected, unforeseen, or the fault of the client.

Moreover, clients need to practice greater patience and restraint when it comes to understanding the reasons for missteps on a matter. Not all firms are automatically at fault in all circumstances. Just as clients invest time with their firms in discussing their cost estimates and value propositions before a matter begins, so too should they invest an equal amount of time after a matter concludes to review the reasons for success or failure. Both parties owe it to each other not to make assumptions and to be candid and fair in their assessments. Only then can the client and the firm determine whether or not value was truly derived on the matter.

## Unlocking the value of cost estimates

Depending on the complexity of a matter, the work effort that goes into a cost estimate can be significant. Clients recognize this and the value of the information contained in a cost estimate if done correctly. How a law firm has calculated such things as the delegation of its resources (staffing model), quantity of time, work effort, efficiency savings, variance and assumption calculations, communication strategy, AFA calculation, blended rate calculation, cost savings projections, and hourly rate calculation are all individually important for clients looking to analyze and conduct any type of post mortem on how successful a law firm has been in regard to its pricing proposal.

Clients can benefit from data mining historical cost estimate data. In fact, those looking to understand potential legal costs on future matters in specific practice areas or geographic markets can do so by leveraging historical cost estimate data. There is a plethora of data in a law firm's cost estimate that, if analyzed properly, can assist clients (and law firms) with the management of their legal spend, benchmarking, and performance measurement when it comes to managing the delivery of legal services and legal spend.

For many clients, the accuracy and reliability of historical billing data, cost estimate, and RFP data has become increasingly important with regards to their legal spend management strategy. Next to the legal knowledge accumulated by clients in their document management (DM) repositories, many of which contain all of their prized opinions and legal precedents, the quantitative historical data accumulated over many years is just as important as the legal knowledge that exists in a DM system. Historical billing data, timekeeper, AFA, spend, RFP, and finally cost estimate data has become the new holy grail of information for clients looking to control costs or law firms looking to improve efficiencies and profit margins.

Firms and clients that once focused only on legal knowledge and the professionals within their firms have over the past couple of decades increasingly grown to appreciate the value of technology in the legal marketplace. Not only has information technology revolutionized the legal marketplace, so too has the empirical data that has been a byproduct of that revolution.

Many clients today routinely data mine their accounting, matter management, or document repositories, looking for any meaningful information that they can use to manage their processes or business better. Business clients that have invested time and money in e-billing and matter management software now leverage their legal ops teams to make sense of the oceans of billing data they extract from their databases. RFP and cost estimate data, once thought to be irrelevant after a bid process, are now being kept and recycled for data mining purposes.

## What type of insight or strategic advantage can cost estimate data give clients?

For starters, many business groups within large corporate environments that are accountable for their legal spend struggle with forecasting legal costs. Predicting legal costs around projects and mandates has grown especially important as many companies look to cost estimates and historical data to help them control legal mandates and their associated legal costs. Historical cost data gives clients the ability to make more informed and accurate business decisions and financial projections that, without cost estimate data, might otherwise be difficult to achieve.

From a sourcing perspective, historical cost estimate data can help clients to identify the most competitively priced, efficient, cost-conscious, or best staffed law firm. Analyzing previous cost estimate data either manually or by way of AI software affords clients the ability to source legal work to firms that are the most suitable for future mandates, thereby avoiding lengthy and protracted requests for proposal or competitive bid processes. Clients are always looking to fine tune their panel of firms or perhaps to rationalize an already large and extensive list of providers. Utilizing cost estimate data allows clients to conduct cross-firm comparisons to identify firms that will yield the greatest cost benefit and savings for the client. The engagement process with new and even existing firms is another area of benefit for clients looking to leverage cost estimate data as the assignment of matters can be expedited to firms where a client has already agreed to a pricing arrangement that is based on reliable and trustworthy information, thereby eliminating the need for any unnecessary engagement negotiations around pricing.

In the case of large litigation matters, cost estimate data can be used to build out budgets related to milestone tasks or even to identify settlement opportunities (sooner rather than later). Many clients today utilize a combination of their proprietary cost estimate and legal spend data, coupled with forecasting AI software to assist them in designing probability models to better assist them with their settlement strategies.

I believe that the value of cost estimate data, or any legal spend data for that matter, cannot be understated and should not be ignored. The analysis of cost estimate data brings with it a discipline in thinking and decision making that has traditionally not existed in the legal marketplace until fairly recently. Leveraging any type of historical spend data or budget data allows the information to "speak" to the client and guide them in their decision-making process.

Moreover, I think that there is a greater uniformity of thought amongst progressive law departments that successful cost estimate strategies and the data that is derived from the process is empowering for not only the client but for firms that strive and invest in being extremely cost competitive and efficient. However, it's important to note that, with all its benefits, data alone does not make the business decisions. Instead, good cost estimate data also empowers the client to make better decisions around the management of their matters, provides greater transparency and assurance that value will be delivered and confirms their decision in having selected the most cost competitive or efficient firm.

## How clients track the success of a cost estimate

Depending on the complexity of a matter, the work effort that goes into a cost estimate can be significant. Clients recognize this and the importance and the value of the information contained in the cost estimate. How a law firm has calculated such things as the delegation of its resources (staffing model), quantity of time, work effort, efficiency savings, variance and assumption calculations, communication strategy, AFA calculation, blended rate calculation, cost savings projections, and hourly rate calculation are all individually important analytics for clients looking to analyze and conduct a post mortem measurement of how successful a law firm has been in regards to its pricing proposal.

For many clients, the accuracy and reliability of historical billing data, cost estimates, and RFP data has become increasingly important with regards to a client's spend management strategy. Next to the legal knowledge accumulated by clients in their document repositories, many of which contain all of their prized opinions and legal precedents, the quantitative historical data accumulated over many years is just as important as the legal knowledge that exists in a DM system.

Historical billing data, timekeeper, AFA, spend, RFP, and finally cost estimate data has become the new holy grail for clients looking to control costs or law firms looking to improve efficiencies and profit margins. Firms and clients that once focused only on legal knowledge and the professionals within their firms have, over the last couple of decades, increasingly grown to appreciate the value of technology in the legal marketplace. Not only has information technology revolutionized the legal marketplace, so too has the empirical data that has been a byproduct of that revolution.

Clients looking to leverage historical cost estimate data will typically leverage the software systems that house their legal spend data. This typically involves collecting various forms of data from a variety of software and AI tools using different business processes and resources.

Perhaps the most useful of these data tools is legal e-billing software that contains an abundance of data points such as timekeeper hourly rate, AFAs, and budget data that can be sorted and analyzed using a multitude of query filters by which the data points can be sliced and diced to produce a variety of reports. Over time many e-billing systems can accumulate an abundance of budget proposals connected to a variety of matters and practice groups involving many firms. This is a treasure trove of information that clients can data mine, analyze and reconcile against actual billings that the client has paid for. This type of cost estimate data can help clients measure the success ratio of proposed budgets against actual billings specific to matters or practice groups.

All of this can empower clients to source legal work to the most reliable and cost effective firms. Clients can also use this data to help them measure law firm performance, even individual timekeeper statistics or task based performance, against actual law firm billings.

Matter management and document management software can also contain various data elements such as cost estimate and budget performance set against calendar dates, measuring the quantity of time, tasks and diarized and scheduled milestones on a matter. Furthermore, the diary functionality that exists in most matter management systems can help clients evaluate the cost of matters over time when measured against certain legal outcomes. This can be used to gauge law firm performance and can be incorporated into how a client measures the overall performance of a law firm. This is especially true on litigation matters where metrics can be established to help clients understand costs associated with milestone events on a matter. This coupled again with billing data can help clients be better prepared knowing when to settle matters and for how much to help mitigate against costly litigation costs.

Collecting the right cost estimate data is only one part of the equation. Report writing and analysis is just as important. Interpreting the data and understanding the impact of the data on the future, implementing strategies to mitigate cost increases and changing law firm behavior are all byproducts of what cost data analysis can deliver and achieve.

By utilizing cross functional internal resources, such as data analysts, finance, procurement and accounting folks clients can conducting proper and thorough data analysis of cost estimate historical data. These resources, as well as legal ops folks, add tremendous value in finding trends, benchmarks and creating forecasts related to legal spend. Not only are clients using cost data to forecast cost savings, cost containment is also a primary focus of many in-house legal teams. Cost estimate data can help clients make the right decisions in hiring the right firms at the right price, empower clients to negotiate favorable pricing to contain costs, stay off increases in legal spend and even help with hiring internal resources.

## Tracking the success of cost estimates

Analyzing law firm billing data attributable to staffing models found in cost estimates empowers clients to move legal work away from firms that rely too heavily on overpriced partners. Instead, clients can require that firms ensure that legal work is more evenly distributed to mid-level associates who are less costly. I have provided an example of an analytical report (Figure 10) that a client can utilize to better understand the staffing ratio and breakdown (at a macro level) amongst several firms using the total dollars billed by each firm. This chart identifies the firms that have, over a two-year period, utilized their (less expensive) associate class more than their partner class. Ideally, such a report can help clients to source legal work to firms that are less costly and/or working their matters more efficiently.

Clients can also use this data to help them measure law firm performance, even individual timekeeper statistics, or task-based performance, against actual law firm billings.

Matter management and document management software can also contain various data elements such as cost estimate and budget performance set against calendar dates, measuring the quantity of time, tasks, and diarized and scheduled milestones on a matter. Furthermore, the diary functionality that exists in most matter management systems can help clients evaluate the cost of matters over time when measured against certain legal outcomes. This can be used to gauge law firm performance and can be incorporated into how a client measures the overall performance of a law firm. This is especially true on litigation matters where metrics can be established to help clients understand costs associated with milestone events on a matter. This, coupled again with billing data, can help clients be better prepared, knowing when to settle matters and for how much to help mitigate against costly litigation costs.

Collecting the right cost estimate data is only one part of the equation. Report writing and analysis is just as important. Interpreting the data and understanding the impact of the data on the future, implementing strategies to mitigate cost increases, and changing law firm behavior are all byproducts of what cost data analysis can deliver and achieve.

By utilizing cross-functional internal resources such as data analysts, finance, procurement, and accounting, clients can conduct proper and thorough data analysis of cost estimate historical data. These resources, as well as legal ops, add tremendous value in finding trends, benchmarks, and creating forecasts related to legal spend. Not only are clients using cost data to forecast cost savings, cost containment is also a primary focus of many in-house legal teams.

## Staffing Ratio Historical Analysis

| Arbor LLP | Partner | | Associate | | Other | | |
|---|---|---|---|---|---|---|---|
| | Total Billed | % of Total Spend | Total Billed | % of Total Spend | Total Billed | % of Total Spend | Total Billed |
| 2016 | 1,476,886 | 43% | 1,730,440 | 50% | 225,571 | 7% | 3,432,897 |
| 2017 | 2,253,663 | 41% | 3,038,143 | 55% | 255,714 | 5% | 5,547,520 |
| 2018 | 1,205,459 | 40% | 1,644,360 | 54% | 179,452 | 6% | 3,029,272 |

| JKL Law | Partner | | Associate | | Other | | |
|---|---|---|---|---|---|---|---|
| | Total Billed | % of Total Spend | Total Billed | % of Total Spend | Total Billed | % of Total Spend | Total Billed |
| 2016 | 70,463 | 26% | 73,354 | 27% | 126,444 | 47% | 270,261 |
| 2017 | 73,686 | 21% | 157,134 | 45% | 116,594 | 34% | 347,414 |
| 2018 | 567,673 | 76% | 112,582 | 15% | 62,501 | 8% | 742,756 |

| Schlitz Cur | Partner | | Associate | | Other | | |
|---|---|---|---|---|---|---|---|
| | Total Billed | % of Total Spend | Total Billed | % of Total Spend | Total Billed | % of Total Spend | Total Billed |
| 2016 | 1,835,399 | 63% | 885,000 | 30% | 198,549 | 7% | 2,918,949 |
| 2017 | 2,110,417 | 59% | 1,112,002 | 31% | 339,656 | 10% | 3,562,074 |
| 2018 | 2,287,602 | 59% | 1,384,771 | 35% | 237,385 | 6% | 3,909,758 |

| Vivendi Law | Partner | | Associate | | Other | | |
|---|---|---|---|---|---|---|---|
| | Total Billed | % of Total Spend | Total Billed | % of Total Spend | Total Billed | % of Total Spend | Total Billed |
| 2016 | 2,436,189 | 54% | 1,687,073 | 37% | 414,648 | 9% | 4,537,910 |
| 2017 | 2,537,826 | 55% | 1,547,265 | 33% | 534,956 | 12% | 4,620,047 |
| 2018 | 4,368,613 | 56% | 2,680,780 | 34% | 800,144 | 10% | 7,849,537 |

| Low & Low | Partner | | Associate | | Other | | |
|---|---|---|---|---|---|---|---|
| | Total Billed | % of Total Spend | Total Billed | % of Total Spend | Total Billed | % of Total Spend | Total Billed |
| 2016 | 1,493,969 | 66% | 685,592 | 30% | 74,772 | 3% | 2,254,333 |
| 2017 | 2,428,447 | 65% | 881,236 | 24% | 411,944 | 11% | 3,721,627 |
| 2018 | 830,179 | 51% | 448,958 | 27% | 359,411 | 22% | 1,638,548 |

| Farber Daz | Partner | | Associate | | Other | | |
|---|---|---|---|---|---|---|---|
| | Total Billed | % of Total Spend | Total Billed | % of Total Spend | Total Billed | % of Total Spend | Total Billed |
| 2016 | 2,295,925 | 69% | 844,794 | 26% | 166,035 | 5% | 3,306,754 |
| 2017 | 2,377,522 | 64% | 1,139,452 | 30% | 223,174 | 6% | 3,740,147 |
| 2018 | 2,657,693 | 60% | 1,319,624 | 30% | 431,424 | 10% | 4,408,741 |

[1] Billing data includes fees, disbursements, taxes for all litigation defence matters (2018-2019) as they relate to timekeeper hourly rate information. Data excludes alternative fee arrangements.

**Optimal Staffing Strategy**

**Cost-conscious and efficient firms looking to add value to their client relationship should (whenever possible) be increasingly delegating work from the partner class to the associate class. Evidence of this can best be illustrated by analyzing law firm staffing ratio data over a historical period.**

**Optimal Staffing Strategy Practices:**

- **As the associate and other class increases in experience and knowledge, so too should the utilization rate for those classes (e.g. utilization ratio for associate/other should indicate continous growth over time).**
- **If the associate staffing utilization ratio is not increasing year over year and it is lower or stagnant (yr/yr) when compared to the partner class, clients need to understand how to improve or reverse this trend with the firm.**
- **Clients should reward firms that indicate higher associate and other staffing and utilization ratios.**
- **Understand what factors and variances drive the partner utilization ratio to increase. Can any of these factors be mitigated or controlled?**
- **Understand how to improve associate over partner utilization ratio.**

***** The firms of Schlitz, Low and Farber stand out to be continously reducing their partner utilization ratio in favor of associate and/or other classes. *****

*Figure 10: Staffing ratio historical analysis.*

of a matter, and especially implement a cost estimate strategy for how it expects to deliver its services and value to the client.

Given what I have seen taking place in recent years in the marketplace, with law firm utilization of various technology tools supported by powerful AI, many experienced firms are in a position to start leveraging forecasting tools and their internal resources to provide accurate forecasting and cost estimate analytics for their clients. Unfortunately, many more firms remain on the sidelines, waiting and hoping that their track record or panel designation will be enough to have their firm selected by the client for the next crisis matter – which is also some of the most lucrative work any firm can be engaged on.

Developing a crisis strategy and a cost estimate framework, even if it's high level, can provide big business clients with a better understanding of what to expect should a crisis legal event occur. Moreover, it also helps to provide an assurance to the client, or potential client, that they have an experienced, prepared tactical legal team waiting in the wings, ready to be deployed with a strategic game plan and a reasonable expectation around costs. All of this is a huge advantage to any big business client. Firms that can pre-emptively provide clients with a holistic strategic plan become, in the eyes of the client, their strategic partner.

The law firm crisis plan should leverage the firm's historical experience on similar types of extraordinary matters, individual knowledge capital, expertise from its best legal professionals, and of course a financial breakdown detailing cost estimate options that offer flexibility as circumstances or variances change.

I have seen many clients, even the most sophisticated in terms of data analysis and cost consciousness, miss this type of cost estimate opportunity with the firms that regularly service them. Clients who get engrossed in black swan matters typically will throw tons of money at legal resources to respond defensively. It is only after the dust has settled and the matter comes to a close does anyone ever question if things could have been done more expeditiously, differently, or more cost effectively. Yes, clients will remember that a firm assisted with mitigating a large issue for them, but they will also be focused on the large expenditures that went with it. Firms want to be in a position to explain their approach, their work, and not have to be questioned about their efficiency. In today's marketplace, there will always be someone in a board room who asks if there was another firm who could have done it cheaper. Firms want the quality of their work to speak for itself, but having that backed up with a detailed crisis plan and cost estimate framework provides added comfort for the firm and ultimately the client,

## How firms should leverage cost estimate data for the their clients

For years I have advocated a proactive approach when managing and containing legal costs in regard to extraor matters. Clients consider these type of matters as black swan happen (thankfully) infrequently but due to their nature are in size, pose a significant legal or reputational risk to the clie exceptionally expensive in terms of legal costs.

Large (big business) companies, because of the nature of ness, are more prone then others to attract black swan event frequency (e.g. insurance, retail, financial services, the mar industries). More often than not, big business typically re extraordinary legal matters in a defensive posture, lining up external legal resources as quickly as possible in order to m crisis or risk to their company.

Most general counsel at big business companies are fo getting the best legal assistance (regardless of cost) as soon as p order to mitigate any reputational or financial impact to their It is understandable then why something like legal costs or to control them quickly disappears as many general counsel board of directors want the crisis or matter to go away as c possible, regardless of the cost. When crisis or black swan eve cost estimates are not high on the list of priorities for most CEO Their primary focus is on mitigating financial damage to the its reputation, investor confidence, or the impact of any eve company's bottom line. Hardly objectives that one can argue a

Still, I believe that there is plenty of opportunity in today's ma for firms, especially panel firms, to step up and become more in their servicing strategies by demonstrating a greater commi their relationship with big business clients. Firms should che status on a panel and ask themselves, "How can we ensure tha our client's first choice (the 'go to firm') the next time they expe crisis or black swan event?"

I believe the answer lies in the firm's ability to be proactive an a strategic "crisis plan" that a big business client will want to when they experience a crisis event. Of course, a cost estimate work should be part of any crisis plan, even though the cost e may have to be customized to the specific facts and business r of each client. Demonstrating a proactive approach for extrao matters provides existing and potential clients with a greater ass that a firm is prepared to take on work and effectively manage all a that when the dust settles on a black swan matter, no one is second guessing anything.

Having a cost estimate designed in advance and specifically for an extraordinary event not only helps the client but also the firm in ensuring that they become the client's first choice next time another crisis event unfolds.

**How can a firm win work on the basis of a cost estimate?**

I have said this before, and it's worth repeating, that firms looking to distinguish themselves from their competitors on the basis of a cost estimate should never assume that they are the only firm that has received a cost estimate proposal. Whether the firm is on a client's panel or being approached by a client for the very first time, it should always approach every cost proposal as if it is participating in a competitive bid situation. As discussed earlier, I have started to see some clients using the cost estimate strategy to source legal work instead of a formalized RFP pricing bid scenario, so that there is an increasing likelihood that clients will issue multiple cost estimates on a matter – unbeknownst to the participating firms.

If after a law firm has done its due diligence and developed what it thinks to be a very competitive price (backed up of course by the math), what else can a firm do to ensure that its cost estimate proposal is accepted by the client?

A winning cost estimate proposal begins with understanding the needs of the client and what it is that they are looking for, either on the matter or in terms of a longer strategic partnership. Many firms make the mistake of treating a cost estimate as only a numbers game, focusing a great deal of their attention on just the price or cost component of their services and less attention on the value added services component, which is just as important and should be given equal consideration. Firms should try to understand the client's needs, beyond the cost component, and look to understand what other value indicators on a matter are important to the client and how the firm can distinguish itself from other cost estimates that the client will receive. This understanding allows the firm an opportunity to gain insights into what the firm can deliver in terms of true value for the client. This in the end may help distinguish a firm from other competing bids.

True value can come from an assortment of things, such as:

- Demonstrating how a firm works efficiently by leveraging technology, AI, and knowledge capital, and recycling legal information and expertise for the benefit of the client, thereby saving the client money and delivering the firm's services more expediently;

- Focusing on internal efficiencies and managing resources effectively through proper staffing, which helps demonstrate how a firm will manage a matter in order for the firm to deliver on its service commitments and value;
- Understanding the client's business model and having institutional knowledge of the client's business strategy and risk appetite;
- Sharing of mutual beliefs around corporate ethics, diversity, and environmental responsibility; and
- Providing the client with an assurance and predictable outcome of the matter, including price.

All of these value indicators are unique to a firm's make-up in the cost estimate proposal and outside of any empirical data that is asked for by the client. Not that the data is not valuable – it is – but the ultimate value of a cost estimate is measured by the client's belief in the firm's ability to deliver on its commitment. The cost estimate proposal is the roadmap to that end in helping the client understand and believe that they have hired the right firm for the right matter.

## When are cost estimates a waste of time and not necessary?

For some clients, depending on the practice area, complexity of the matter, or even the risk appetite of the client, going through the exercise of completing a thorough cost estimate may just not be worth the effort. Despite all of the benefits attributable to the cost estimate process, it does take some work on the part of the client and law firm. Clients need to consider the practicality of their situations and weigh whether or not it makes sense to invest time and energy in the process.

Below are some potential circumstances in which clients (and law firms) may find that a cost estimate may not be worth the investment of time and resources.

### Transactional, routine and straightforward matters

Many companies will require legal assistance from external law firms in specific practice areas of the law that are highly transactional, routine, and straightforward. Legal costs associated with such practice areas as litigation defense or plaintiff, collection recovery litigation, insurance, employment, immigration, or intellectual property type matters tend to be predictable and straightforward and clients will typically use the same firm (repeatedly) for the same type of matter. Cost estimates for repetitive type matters where there is a mutual understanding by all parties involved as to the work effort and what each matter costs is not cost efficient and unnecessary.

### Predictable matters with little risk of variances

Matters that are highly predictable, reoccur with regular frequency, and where there is little risk of any variances occurring offer clients a straightforward opportunity to manage these type of matters without a cost estimate. Because of the recurring and predictable nature of the legal matters, a negotiated flat fee or fixed fee arrangement with the law firm is perhaps the best and easiest approach a client can utilize. In these types of scenarios a cost estimate would not be required.

### Historical AFAs

Many clients utilize an assortment of AFAs with their law firms and are very comfortable with the pricing arrangements negotiated in the AFA. Consequently, clients may not have a need to look past their AFAs for greater transparency. If the AFAs are amenable to the client's needs, the matter is transactional in nature and/or there is little risk to the client of any variances interfering with an existing matter, this is another scenario where a client would not have any reason to embark on a cost estimate approach.

### Tight deadlines

Business demands on clients are always changing, including shifting timelines for business deliverables and project tasks. In a fast-paced corporate environment where there are tight deadlines, there may not always be the luxury of time to allow a client to conduct a proper cost assessment or pricing analysis for a potential legal matter. In other circumstances, clients may simply require a quick opinion in support of a strategy to either close a deal or to respond to a regulatory body. Whatever the scenario, time may be of the essence and the client may have no other option than to simply trust the firm (without any supporting analysis) on what the cost will be. I have seen multiple instances of this scenario play out at large companies and in almost every example the panel firm did not disappoint the client and was trusted to bill fairly for the services that it provided. In the rare instances where a firm was found to be extremely expensive or the client adversely surprised by the total cost of the matter, the firm was not a panel firm, was located in a foreign jurisdiction, or had no historical ties to the client.

### Leveraging historical cost data

Clients who have been utilizing and storing historical spend, cost, and RFP/bid data have a significant advantage when it comes to managing their legal spend. As discussed in previous sections of this book, data today is empowering to those who know what they are looking for and know how to use it to manage their business affairs. Some clients may not have a need to start new cost estimates if they already have the benefit of relatively recent (i.e. within the past 12 months) cost estimates for similar matters. Whenever possible, clients, as well as firms, should try to leverage historical information for efficiency purposes. Many times clients are involved on repetitive type legal transactions that rarely change, so that cost estimates if required can be used as a benchmark to gauge predictability and forecasting, thereby eliminating the need for new cost estimates.

### Low cost matters

There will inevitably be some legal matters where the expected cost of the matter is low and the matter is uncomplicated and very straightforward. For those types of matters, the client may wish to look to an AFA instead of a rigorous and methodical cost estimate approach.

### Too many variances

Clients will typically utilize cost estimates on large, complicated legal matters where legal costs are expected to be significant. I have encountered numerous situations where, ironically, a legal matter was too complicated and required many variables and assumptions that in the end made the cost estimate unreliable and ultimately unrealistic. Clients may encounter similar circumstances where a matter may not be worth the effort to implement a cost estimate that will repeatedly have to be revised. Examples of this can occur in situations where a client may have to negotiate the terms of a vendor contract, a litigation action may take an abrupt turn and introduce unforeseen legal issues impacting timelines and resulting in unforeseen delays, or even a situation where matter scope may change abruptly due to unpredictable market conditions or a client's business strategy changing course. All of these are examples that may significantly derail any well thought out cost estimate. If a client knows full well that something substantive may impact the overall cost estimate, they may think twice about investing their and their law firm's time in a cost estimate. In such circumstances, clients might be better off agreeing to simple hourly rate caps and regular updates on legal costs should the matter be protracted instead of implementing a formalized cost estimate plan that may be of little value to all parties involved.

## Who cares about the math, show me the value

The header title is a somewhat cynical statement and may be true for a few very sophisticated legal departments and legal ops experts, but not for the overwhelming majority of clients struggling to control and contain external legal costs. Not every client is at the high end of the legal operation spectrum where a few have been fortunate enough to enjoy a utopian partnership with their law firms.

It is rare to see that level of faith and trust across an entire panel of firms, but not uncommon to see clients enjoy such a valuable relationship with a select few legal partners on their panel. I personally have only seen it a few times in my 20-year career.

Where a strategically valued partnership exists, it has not come overnight but rather over a period of time, multiple matters, hundreds of hours of billable time, and most importantly, an honest and highly communicative relationship.

The journey to value doesn't have to take a client through a myriad of data analysis and years of testing AFAs with firms. It can begin by establishing a mutual understanding of how the client expects to receive its services (i.e. delivery), the quality of the legal advice, the cost, and finally the benefit of that advice to the client.

The math behind any comprehensive cost estimate is still important and should not be disregarded as suggested in the title header. From a profitability perspective, how law firms reach a pricing conclusion is not only important to themselves but also to the client, whether or not they ask for the backup and analysis (i.e. "the math"). The due diligence a firm invests in a cost estimate exercise helps the firm to understand how the client's matter will be managed. The cost component of the estimate in effect becomes the basis or framework by which other value indicators are governed.

Staffing, resource cost, disbursements, AFAs, delivery timetable, variances, and assumptions are all value indicators that are related to price. The firm is obligated to stay within the parameters of its cost estimate to ensure that the final work product delivered to the client is of value.

However, there is one factor that risks undermining any cost estimate strategy or value proposition that a firm puts forward – suboptimal legal advice or work product.

I have focused very little attention in this book on how the quality of legal services delivered by a firm impacts the overall strategy of a matter and the integrity of a cost estimate. Needless to say, it is significant and critical to the engagement. After all, what good is a cost estimate if the work product is shabby? The client won't care about any cost estimate, they will be extremely dissatisfied and probably never hire the firm again. Oh, and they might also decide not to pay the bill.

My assumption throughout this book has been that clients have done their homework before engaging their firm. Whether that firm is on their panel or a new off the street firm, the client is confident based on their own intelligence that the firm is more than capable of providing them with excellent legal advice. I will not do a deep analysis on how the client came to that conclusion, but only say that this unfortunately is not always the case. Ask any client and they will tell you stories about how they misjudged or were misled by the expertise they thought existed at a particular firm and how they were dissatisfied by the quality of legal services that were provided to them.

I believe that "the math" is an important component when there is a determination to be made about value. I have said this before and it is worth repeating that cost only becomes an issue and problematic when the client questions the value of the services that have been provided. How those services have been provided and what governs the pricing framework for their delivery is found in the cost estimate. In the end, the law firm's math impacts the price of its services being quoted in the cost estimate and all of the other value indicators influence the client's determination of value.

### Is there any room for an "instinctive approach" on a cost estimate?

Some seasoned lawyers will tell you that they don't need a formalized cost estimate plan to tell them how to price their legal work because they have been doing it for years and instinctively know how to price their work. This constituency of lawyers has relied primarily on their expertise, historical experience and mostly gut feelings in order to provide estimates for their clientele. Rarely, if ever, have they had a need to utilize data analysis software or the finance department in any formalized analytical practices as described in this book. The "instinctive approach" has served them well, but its days are numbered as most firms understand that clients today want estimates backed up by real empirical data and not just "gut feelings".

Even the small pocket of lawyers at firms that still utilize the instinctive approach have now succumbed to market pressures and understand that, on the larger significant matters, it's in their (and their law firm's) best financial interest to double check their instinctive approach against some of the firm's real historical data. Often this responsibility rests with the firm's legal ops or finance experts who ensure that any subjective estimate gets validated against the firm's real financial data. Moreover, if there is a data delta between the real data and the instinctive approach, the lawyer must ensure that the gap is closed as much as possible before anything in terms of a formal cost estimate goes out the door to the client.

The data delta can be attributable to such things as changing market conditions, cost of living, economic variables, preferred client discounts – even AFAs and variances can all come into play on a matter and may in some way impact a cost estimate analysis. An instinctive approach is unlikely to accommodate many of these factors thereby leaving the lawyer in a risky situation if their instinctive estimate results in an overage.

While some lawyers may argue that there is nothing wrong with the instinctive approach and it has served them well, I believe the opposite. Clients today are demanding greater assurances and informed decisions around legal costs. While many want the most experienced legal expert on their matters, they don't want to take subjective "guesstimates" to their GC or the board of directors on a large M&A deal or class action. Client expectations are high and they expect that whatever the firm provides can be supported by real empirical information. Subjective estimates cannot provide the level of granularity and specificity that real empirical cost estimates can. Moreover, instinctive estimates cannot accurately account for variances and assumptions which, most times, if they do occur, may result in the firm having to write-down or "eat" legal costs.

As the legal industry continues to change, fewer lawyers are relying on instinct and more on their legal ops folks and their data analytics and empirical-based truisms as the basis for providing cost estimates for their clients. Although the instinctive approach still has a beating pulse, its lifecycle is quickly approaching an end as legal work of every type is growing closer to becoming increasingly commoditized, predictable, and supported by value propositions based on real performance data driven by AI.

Clients are increasingly demanding greater comfort and assurances around costs that are supported by reliable data and analysis. The instinctive approach may appear to provide some level of value, but it is all dependent on the lawyer's subjective opinion. Cost estimates on the other hand provide the greatest comfort as well as a defined (objective) framework for ensuring the delivery of value in an engagement.

# Chapter 5:
# Other considerations

## How third party "pass through" hourly rates impact a cost estimate

In a free market economy, firms can charge their clients whatever they like, but more times than not, firms decide based on supply and demand. For decades, many firms have utilized a dual scale of rates – one that they charge for large corporations and institutional buyers, and another for third parties, referred to as "pass through" costs. Firms that know in advance that their clients will be paying the bill tend to get preferred (i.e. heavily discounted) pricing if the client is paying the legal costs directly. However, a higher (premium) rate is charged to the client if the legal cost is not borne by the client but "passed through" to a third party and the third party is paying the bill.

Pass through premium rates charged to third parties can be as much as 30 to 40 percent higher than discounted rates. Depending on the market – New York or London – the premium may be even higher. Given the large delta between the two rate scales, the utilization of premium rates in a cost estimate may have a huge impact on a client's budget. Clients who are unaware of the dual scale billing practice may unknowingly be charged a large premium if they accept a firm's proposal without confirming which rate scale was used to calculate the cost proposal.

Collection recovery matters are a good example of pass through billing where a financial institution hires a law firm to commence a collection recovery against a debtor for defaulting on a credit card debt. The litigation costs ultimately will be paid by the debtor (i.e. third party). The third party pays a higher hourly rate and consequently higher total cost than if it were just the client paying the firm directly. This practice also tends to be the norm quite frequently on commercial financing, capital markets, or investment financing transactions. Different governing bodies, law societies, and even clients have different rules around how to manage dual (premium) rates charged to third party clients. Many clients have (for reputational reasons) decided to maintain a relationship with a firm that honors one set of rates and if the client enjoys the benefit of a discounted hourly rate, that discount is also afforded to any third parties that the client deals with on a legal transaction, regardless of the type of legal action the client is involved in.

From a cost estimate perspective, clients should confirm with their firm whether or not it has utilized premium hourly rates when calculating fixed fee or flat fee cost estimate proposals for the client. A firm may have intentionally utilized a premium hourly rate if it knew in advance that a third party was going to pay for the legal costs instead of the client. In such circumstances, obviously the cost estimate that the firm received would be higher due to the premium. I have also seen numerous scenarios, particularly involving larger firms, where the firm accidentally utilized its premium rates instead of its discounted rates on its cost estimate quote. Some firms are large organizations with many different folks working on multiple matters at once so it's not uncommon to see a disconnect between a lawyer and their billing or finance folks where cost estimates may involve multiple professionals.

Clients should also beware of firms looking to support the utilization of premium rates by claiming it is written into the firm's billing policy which supports a "special" rate structure carved out for certain practice groups or types of matters. Unfortunately, dual rates still appear to be common practice in many major markets around the globe. It is up to the client to manage its reputation and that of its firms against such questionable inter-law firm billing guidelines.

## Treating cost estimates like a request for proposal (RFP) bid

Considering the hyper-competitiveness that exists amongst law firms and alternative legal service providers in today's legal marketplace, it would not be a stretch to say that firms should treat cost estimates like they treat competitive pricing bids or RFPs. If a matter is complicated, I would expect a firm's cost estimate to be as thorough and analytical as if the firm were preparing a response to an RFP bid. Therefore, both the quality of the analysis and the level of preparation a firm would ordinarily dedicate to an RFP response should also be applied to a firm's cost estimate proposal.

RFP bids and cost estimate proposals share many of the same analytical components. Both processes ultimately end up as pricing proposals in front of clients who are looking for cost certainty, competitiveness, and transparency on the matters for which they engage external counsel. Clients that regularly conduct RFP bids for panel firms have moved away from complicated RFP bids and focused greater attention on value indicators and pricing, so that much of the information contained in an RFP and the analytical preparation that goes into an RFP bid can and should be applied to a cost estimate proposal.

It is understandable why a firm may want to focus a great deal of attention on the pricing and cost information contained in a cost estimate, but there are also other areas of importance that clients look to aside from the pricing information contained in a cost estimate. One of of the key areas of an RFP starts with understanding and defining the scope of the engagement. For obvious reasons, this is by far one of the most critical components of any RFP and likewise a cost estimate bid proposal. All too often I have seen firms provide bid proposals that were based on assumptions because they were either too modest or too proud to ask a client for assistance in clarifying the definition around the scope of an engagement. The consequences of not speaking up and making risky assumptions regarding scope may leave a firm at a significant cost disadvantage to those firms that do ask for scope clarity or communicate questions around how to deal with variances.

Other value indicators such as defined business requirements, communication, timeliness, AFA options, variance strategies, staffing, disbursements, third party assistance, even things like code of conduct and service level commitments, have begun to appear in cost estimate strategies proposed by clients.

Obviously, the pricing component of any cost proposal that a firm puts forward is of utmost importance, but so too should be the understanding that a cost estimate proposal is very much like a competitive RFP bid. Firms should never assume that they are the only ones that have been approached to submit a cost estimate bid for a particular matter.

Many clients have in fact started to utilize their standardized cost estimate templates as abbreviated mini-RFP bids. It is not uncommon for many in-house legal teams today to conduct a cost estimate exercise with multiple panel firms in order to satisfy the needs of internal business partners or to make a quick determination to source legal work without the administrative burden of a large RFP process. Consequently, a firm's ability to distinguish its cost estimate from other competing law firms is just as important as if the firm were competing in a more formalized RFP process. Firms that understand this recognize that legal servicing is no longer just about the practice of law and legal advice but is also about the business of law.

Meeting client expectations around how they want to be serviced and pay for their legal services will help a firm enjoy market advantage over their peers. This is especially true in today's legal marketplace which has become increasingly homogenized where many firms look alike, are doing the same things, offering the same services at the same price.

Cost estimates, like RFPs, offer firms a fundamental yet excellent opportunity to distinguish themselves from others while also profiling a firm's value proposition. If a firm can learn how to leverage the right internal resources, create processes around data analysis, and ultimately package their information into a standardized framework that is straightforward, transparent, and easy for a client to understand, they will stand out amongst their peers and improve their profitability.

Moreover, clients also expect that the cost estimates they accept are practical, realistic, and can be supported with an assurance that the firm will stand by its proposal. I have experienced numerous cost estimate occasions where firms attempted to back-pedal on their agreed pricing arrangements. In almost all of those circumstances clients have held their ground and refused to grant any latitude to allow a firm to revise and increase its cost proposal after it has already been submitted and accepted by the client.

This last point speaks to the importance of ensuring that a firm has done its due diligence in regard to its cost analysis and understanding the practicality of its proposals. Therefore, firms should approach cost estimates with the same level of due diligence and finality as an RFP bid. Once a cost estimate has been submitted to a client, firms should not be looking to take it back, revise, amend, or supplement the cost proposal with supporting information or documents, unless of course the client prompts the firm to do so.

Clients expect that what they receive is in fact a final proposal and that the firm will honor and stand by that proposal. If a firm has made a mistake, misunderstood the scope or client's business requirements or instructions – so be it. I have dealt with communication in an earlier chapter, but it is worth repeating that the onus rests on the firm to ensure that it has properly understood all of the client's instructions and has asked any and all necessary questions prior to submitting a cost estimate proposal. This is no different to what would occur in an RFP scenario. Having said that, there is always room for negotiation, but only if the client invites the changes to the proposal. Unfortunately for firms, I have never seen a client wanting to negotiate a cost proposal up from what a firm originally proposed.

## The importance of trust in cost estimates

Do clients trust the cost estimates that law firms propose?

There is no way around it other than to be perfectly blunt – many clients have for years distrusted firms around pricing and how they bill for their services. There is a myriad of reasons for this, but I think that many corporate clients and their in-house legal teams will point to suboptimal service delivery as the principal root cause around a client's reasons for distrust.

I think many firms, if they are truly honest with themselves, will admit that they have been slow to adopt some of the most basic tenets of the client service industry, such as proactive communication, timeliness, reliability, affordability, efficiency, effectiveness, and value. Firms have progressively been getting better, but for many, service delivery continues to be a challenge as it takes a back seat to other economic factors such as profitability and watching margins. For many clients, the tenets of service delivery are fundamentally supported by a belief and trust in the firm they engage. Trust is just as important as the cost for legal services.

Earlier in the book I discussed the distrust that has plagued the legal industry for years, because of its penchant for a billing model that is incentivized by profit and not quality or value. This then begs the question that if clients can't trust firms on what and how they bill using hourly rates, then how can a client trust a firm on the cost estimate that they propose?

The issue of distrust speaks volumes in the preceding question and especially for cynical clients, who believe that there is very little value in pursuing a cost estimate because firms generally can't be trusted – end of story. They can't be trusted to provide any level of transparency; they can't be trusted to provide reliable and truthful data; they will not honor their commitment, etc. If it's so bad, then where does that leave the client? My response is that, if it's that bad, then it is not a relationship, but merely a transaction being exchanged multiple times without any interest in each party's wellbeing other than to deliver item A (services) in exchange for item B (money). It doesn't even matter if the nature of the engagement is complicated or even a large extraordinary matter such as a black swan event – there is no loyalty or interest in a longer-term relationship; it is just another transaction. Cost in such situations is the only driver, a motivator to deliver "A" in exchange for "B". It's unfortunate, but I still see clients today involved in such transactional situations.

In the transactional scenario, the client will always be at a disadvantage and worried that they are being taken advantage of. The basis of such adversarial transactions is one thing – money. Every matter is questioned, every line item on a bill is second guessed, there are countless discussions about suspected over-billing and over-staffing, disbursements that weren't authorized, instructions that weren't clear enough, work that was not authorized (the list goes on). In short, a lot of time, energy, and resources are expended on dealing with a process that is based on distrust. Nothing ever gets better for the client (and the firm) because the client's bias is fairly implanted. The whole cycle is doomed to fail and unsustainable.

Thankfully, there are more progressive clients on the right side of the relationship spectrum who recognize the importance of service delivery requirements and the value of investing time and resources in proactive cost control practices such as cost estimate strategies. This group of clients, unlike the cynics, will dedicate the energy and resources needed in order to grow a relationship and ensure that there is a level of trust in that relationship. These clients understand that cost estimates afford the client and firm an opportunity to get there, beyond a transactional scenario. Implementing a cost estimate strategy doesn't automatically create a perfect utopia – it takes time and work – but it is certainly an important step that helps clients understand how a firm prices its work and allows the firm to add greater clarity and value to the engagement process.

Lastly, it is worth repeating that price becomes an issue only in the absence of value. I think that more and more law firms have started to recognize that value is determined by the client, who is increasingly looking for greater transparency, supported by historical real data and an assurance that the firm will deliver on its cost estimate. For the client, all of these things reinforce a commitment to greater honesty and trust.

## Challenging a law firm's cost estimate

Clients have come to expect a lot from the firms they engage. It is not surprising then that clients may want to ask questions of a firm to validate certain information or to get a better assurance around a particular aspect of the engagement. I find that this is especially true as it pertains to anything that has to do with the cost or service delivery aspects of a matter. Therefore, firms should expect (and be prepared) to be challenged and questioned by clients who want a higher level of validation and assurance when it comes to a law firm's cost estimate proposal. Moreover, firms should also be prepared that the validation process may result in a negotiation process whereby the client may want the firm to reduce part or all of its cost estimate proposal. Given the legal marketplace today, I believe that every firm should be willing to negotiate to some extent and ultimately make a decision as to what is in its best economic interest and what is viable for the firm to agree to. This might be easier said than done in such a hyper-competitive market where firms may not be in a position to negotiate to maintain profitability. Ultimately, it's up to each firm to decide what is economically viable for itself. At the very least, clients expect firms to be amenable to negotiating. What happens after that is up to both parties.

Clients may have certain expectations around a budget or staffing model and should make every effort to ensure that the firm understands the client's requirements before the firm submits its cost estimate. Communicating business requirements or expectations to a firm at the time of engagement is critically important as it provides accurate information for the firm to create a reliable cost estimate and reduces the risk for having to make adjustments to the cost estimate down the road because one party omitted some information.

Clients looking to validate the components of a cost estimate proposal should ensure that the:

- Scope of engagement has been properly defined and explained, including definitions relating to specific tasks or milestones;
- Law firm staffing model matches the appropriate experience of resources with the complexity of a matter;
- Final cost estimate used to negotiate final pricing is realistic and includes or excludes a variance cushion as needed;
- Deliverable dates for milestones or tasks are realistic and mutually acceptable; and
- Communication strategy is clearly defined and mutually agreed at the outset of a matter.

If at any time a client or a law firm is uncertain about any element or component of the cost estimate, they should address the matter with the other party.

Below are listed a few questions a client should consider asking a law firm in the course of validating a cost estimate proposal:

- What hourly rates were used to calculate the cost estimate?
- Were there any variances included, and if so, what percentage of the cost estimate reflects the variance cushion?

- What is the logic around the firm's variance cushion, and how will it be utilized?
- How was the allotment of time determined for each professional working on the matter?
- Was the allotment of time based on any historical experience and previous matters?
- Did the firm utilize (i.e. recycle) any previous historical work product in establishing its cost estimate? If not, why not?
- How will the firm deal with variances?
- What guarantee can the law provide that the work product will be delivered on time and on budget?
- What is the plan if there is a delay in delivering the work product?
- Will the law firm write-down a portion of its cost estimate if the firm fails to meet a deadline?

I have rarely heard of a law firm not being receptive to providing a client with additional cost estimate information when a client has asked a firm to clarify things or explain how the firm calculated its cost estimate. Many firms today have an abundance of empirical data and statistics, and they understand the importance of data to their clients.

Any attempt by a law firm to try and avoid providing additional "back-up" cost data, or to justify a cost estimate on the basis of subjective factors or that the firm understands the issue better than the client, or that the cost estimate is reflective of market conditions, should be interpreted as a warning sign to the client.

In today's legal marketplace, clients are demanding transparency and require reliable and accurate information to make informed business decisions. Anything less than transparency and a willingness to discuss a proposal is becoming increasingly unacceptable to many clients because they have zero tolerance for firm pushback or apathy.

It's in the best of interest of a law firm to provide the client with as much information as is necessary in order for the client to make an informed decision and ultimately give them an assurance that the firm's cost estimate is accurate and reasonable. If a client has to question a cost estimate or asks, "Show me the math", it usually indicates that something is offside, not right, or simply that the client needs further comfort in understanding a component of the cost estimate.

I have personally encountered awkward situations where senior partners have had to confess to me that a portion of their cost estimate was based on subjective feelings because certain legal work was "bespoke and could only be quantified as a result of personal historical experience" or simply based on their "gut feeling". This type of explanation may have been permissible many years ago, but in today's data-driven marketplace it is increasingly unpalatable to cost-conscious buyers of legal services. Yes, some work may be complicated with many variables and, in fact, may be bespoke, but that is generally the exception. That is why detailed breakdowns of cost estimates (backed up by real data) are beneficial to both the client and law firm and can help minimize overages and the need for questioning and client challenges.

## How to get a firm to reduce its cost estimate

Cost estimates should be viewed as proposed pricing arrangements that are offered to clients as part of a law firm's engagement. The cost estimate acts as a roadmap for getting the firm to its final destination/objective. Depending on the destination (matter), how a firm proposes its route (tasks, scope, staffing, communication, and pricing) may differ from how the client envisions the path to the final destination.

I believe that in today's legal marketplace clients have the final say in determining whether to accept or decline a cost estimate proposal. If clients have certain budget expectations or restrictions, they should share them at the outset of any initial discussions with the law firm. Firms also have a responsibility for ensuring that they can back up their cost estimates with real data when clients ask to see evidence of how the firm came up with its cost estimate proposals.

Clients should be aware that firms are extremely risk-averse and will present options to mitigate risk for their clients (and themselves). Mitigating risk may require that a firm expands the scope parameters of an engagement, even though the clients may not see it that way. In the end, clients must decide whether economic requirements trump a firm's need to mitigate risk. If the client accepts the risk and is prepared to trade off a low-cost estimate for increased business, litigation, or reputational risk, they must be prepared to accept the risk and repercussions from that decision and not the firm.

Cost-conscious clients that are fiscally prudent will (internally) question almost every cost estimate. A few cynical clients will always view law firms as opportunistic adversaries out to make a buck. Fortunately, sophisticated buyers of legal services understand how to utilize their data, their market, and their history around expected legal costs. They also recognize the value that many quality firms provide. Similarly, those types of clients understand that many firms recognize and understand the needs of their clients and are willing to make price concessions (i.e. always be ready to negotiate) in order to win the work. These types of firms are always amenable to looking at ways to make cost estimates work for their clients.

The following is a list clients can utilize to help them reduce a law firm's cost estimate:

- Define the matter/project scope prescriptively – firms may make assumptions in order to mitigate the risk that a firm sees if instructions are ambiguous or unclear;
- Communicate clearly with the firm to ensure they understand the scope of engagement;
- Confirm if assumptions have been "baked" into a law firm's cost estimate, and if they are relevant or a stretch to mitigate risk? (consider asking that the firm separate them from the cost estimate);
- Reconfirm the staffing utilization ratio that the firm is proposing to use during the engagement – perhaps the firm is over-staffing to cover off for assumptions. Once the assumptions have been removed, the staffing model should also be adjusted accordingly, thereby bringing down the cost estimate;
- Reconfirm deliverables and timelines – some firms may add a premium to their proposed work, assuming the client needs their assistance right away, thereby charging a premium to deliver that work ASAP. If there is no rush, or the client can wait a week or more, perhaps the firm can also make an adjustment in cost;
- Review disbursement costs and request the firm waive disbursement charges – if the firm has included administrative overheads or other types of internal charges to the cost estimate, there may be a case to be made to have these items removed, thereby reducing the overall value of a cost estimate; and
- Risk/reward incentive – although not on its own an element of costs estimates, a firm may be willing to further reduce a proposed cost estimate if it fails to perform a certain way or deliver on a specific milestone task. Conversely, a firm may be expected to be rewarded above a proposed cost estimate if it over-achieves or exceeds expectations as described in the scope of engagement and/or cost estimate.

## What to do when a cost estimate fails

Both parties to a cost estimate should always work to ensure that their cost estimate is as sound and solid as possible. However, even the most well thought-out and comprehensive plans may be unexpectedly derailed by such things as a failure to properly define and communicate the scope of an engagement, underestimating the staffing requirements of a matter, poor service delivery, sudden scope change, or simply making costly assumptions.

Aside from unexpected scope change, cost estimates are more likely to fail because something was missed or one of the parties (or both) strayed from the mutually agreed-upon plan. Invariably, the success or failure of a cost estimate hinges on mutual understanding, buy-in, and the acceptance of both parties to the agreed-upon cost estimate. After all, if the cost estimate is agreed upon, it becomes the pricing arrangement for the terms of engagement; being in conflict with a client's terms puts a firm's status with the client at risk and may result in adverse repercussions.

The best way to deal with a failed cost estimate during a matter is to understand and identify the area of disconnect and, if possible, try to renegotiate the terms and communicate the results to all parties. Ideally, dealing with a sidetracked cost estimate should be done as soon as possible to mitigate any greater repercussions to the matter and perhaps the relationship. This is especially important if both parties are involved in large, protracted, or legally complex matters, which may involve a multitude of tasks and a variety of pricing arrangements that may put the client at risk.

A client and a firm should consider the following list of items should their cost estimate be sidetracked and they run into difficulties:

- Clearly identify the problem with the cost estimate (this could be anything that derails a plan);
- Communicate the issue to all parties involved (internal business partners, clients, in-house counsel, and law firm contacts);
- Propose fair and constructive suggestions;
- Avoid the blame game – focus on the issue and the solution;
- Act quickly and be proactive;
- Do not make assumptions (contact the client or firm for clarification); and
- Learn from this situation to avoid repeating it in the future.

## Billing for a cost estimate

One of the last points that I would like to discuss is the cost of doing business and how law firms have increasingly had to absorb costs associated with a multitude of (sometimes extremely onerous) client requests, including cost estimates. Undeniably, if a cost estimate is done right, it may involve one or more people spending several hours analyzing, aggregating, confirming, and proposing a formal cost estimate to a client. If there are subsequent points of clarification needed or follow up questions to be answered, additional work may be required on the part of a firm – again, perhaps involving multiple individuals. Some firms may think that they have legitimate grounds to be compensated for their work effort on a cost estimate. In many circumstances there is no guarantee that a client will accept a firm's cost proposal, so at the very least a firm may want to ask for some sort of compensation, given all of the work the firm put into producing their cost estimate. I believe that, unless a client has stated otherwise, there is a market-wide assumption that most cost estimates are non-reimbursable expenses.

In my career, I have had very few instances where law firms have approached me to ask for compensation on cost estimates or in pricing bid proposals. Where compensation was permitted for a firm, it was on an exception basis, recognizing a tremendous amount of work on a highly complicated multi-jurisdictional litigation matter. Firms should assume the costs, time, energy, and resources they put into developing a cost estimate is non-recoverable and should be considered as the cost of doing business.

## What is the future for cost estimates?

As the legal marketplace continues to change, so too will the needs of clients and their requirements around service delivery. Clients will increasingly look to automation, AI, and process reengineering for assistance and finding opportunities to increase cost savings and manage their external legal spend better.

To conclude, below are listed 15 changes that I believe may be coming to the legal marketplace with regards to how cost estimates will change for clients and firms:

1. The technology revolution in the legal market will continue, with even more innovation and the utilization of technology tools, analytical software, and artificial intelligence to help clients and firms understand how to price legal work better and offer more accurate forecasting capabilities around variances and assumptions;

2. Increased automation of data analysis tools and better integration capabilities with clients' legal e-billing and matter management systems will take clients far beyond where they are today in managing cost estimate processes. Clients will become liberated as automation will create efficiencies and free up their time;
3. Data analysis software configurability will improve, as will the affordability of these products to bring more analytical tools within reach of all types of clients and firms;
4. Cost estimate templates, if not already automated, will for the majority of clients be replaced with online budget tools that firms will be required to complete and submit online. Clients will be able to utilize online cost estimate bid offerings to multiple law firms at once, receive their returned proposals and, not unlike an RFP process, select the most cost effective firm for their matter;
5. The analytical capabilities of new cost estimate software will allow clients to review a firm's cost proposal and provide feedback in the form of an assessment to the client;
6. Most existing manual cost estimate processes (e.g. excel templates, email forms, question forms, meetings, solicitation for feedback, approvals) will no longer be required as cost estimate software will have built in communication and alert functionality to expedite contacting a firm or business client within the software tool;
7. Cost estimates will be better aligned and integrated with existing market e-billing software in order to allow firms to upload real time WIP and reconcile current workloads against any pricing proposals;
8. Software will report to clients via tickler alerts (SMS or email) that will warn clients of law firms conducting work on variances or assumptions that may be out of scope;
9. Scope will be monitored using advanced activity codes and reported to clients;
10. Firms will be required to upload daily activity codes (e.g. flat fee or fixed fee arrangements) to identify progress on a matter and to help clients understand whether a firm is on time and within their budget;
11. Automation will practically eliminate the risk of any cost overages occurring without the client's electronic approval;

12. Many cost estimate issues that both clients and firms face today will be mitigated by automated compliance monitoring through the entire CE process;
13. Cost estimate software will become more affordable and therefore accessible, empowering legal ops experts in many law departments;
14. Compliance rules in software will be self-configurable and invaluable for clients to monitor their arrangements and mitigate against any overages; and
15. Law firm success, as measured by the work a firm has completed within a cost estimate, will be automatically evaluated by AI and the firm will be graded. Law firm gradings will be downloaded to reports for legal executives to assess performance and for future sourcing activities, and if shared amongst panel firms, to foster a more competitive community and incentivize law firm performance.

I believe emphasis on cost estimates will only increase (with the assistance of automation tools) so much so that they will become table stakes for many clients who are demanding greater transparency around legal costs.

I expect that as corporate clients become more sophisticated in their utilization of cost data, they will continue to search out better ways to manage their legal spend and how they source their legal work. Cost estimates will not disappear but how strategies are operationalized will change.

Mechanically, the delivery mechanisms of how clients and law firms utilize cost estimates may change and become more expedient and efficient. Cost estimates will become the central component of a law firm's value proposition as more clients will require this at the outset of their matters. Without a value proposition, firms may find themselves increasingly challenged to grow market share and attract new clients, many of whom will view such firms as being out of step with market best practices. Cost transparency, excellent service delivery, and qualitative legal services will become absolute table stakes for clients looking for assurances of value in a highly competitive and commoditized marketplace.

## Conclusion

As corporate buyers of legal services grow increasingly perceptive in how they manage their legal costs, they are steadily looking to law firms to deliver transparent value at transparent prices. The cost estimate that a firm proposes to any client must be supported by factual, reliable data that is specific to the client's needs, thereby ensuring that the client will recognize the value of the services that are to be provided. If a firm is presenting a cost estimate to a new client then the challenge increases, and the onus is directly on the firm to ensure that its cost estimate lines up squarely with the client's objectives, is reasonably priced, and that the firm is amenable to negotiating a middle ground should the client want options. In both scenarios, clients want greater visibility and an assurance that they are getting value – and cost savings – for the services the law firm is proposing to provide. Legal service delivery is no longer just about the law but has become more about the delivery, service, and the economics or business of law. Comprehensive and well thought-out cost estimates are the backbone of any engagement and provide the assurance that many clients are looking for in today's hyper-competitive legal marketplace.

www.ingramcontent.com/pod-product-compliance
Ingram Content Group UK Ltd.
Pitfield, Milton Keynes, MK11 3LW, UK
UKHW021849150926
8657IPUK00005B/155

9 781783 583966